The Nanny

The Nanny Handbook

How to find and keep the best nannies and au pairs

KAREN HOUSE AND LOUISE SHEPPARD

SIMON & SCHUSTER
A VIACOM COMPANY

First published in Great Britain by Simon & Schuster UK Ltd, 2001
A Viacom Company

1 3 5 7 9 10 8 6 4 2

Simon & Schuster UK Ltd
Africa House
64–78 Kingway
London WC2B 6AH

Simon & Schuster Australia
Sydney

A CIP catalogue record for this book is available from the British Library

ISBN 0-684-86636-6

Printed and bound in Great Britain by
Butler & Tanner Ltd, Frome and London

For our parents, husbands and children

Contents

Part IV: Managing Your Changing Needs

Acknowledgements

Many people have helped us to put this book together and our thanks go to all those who have spent time answering our questions and providing us with information.

Particular thanks go to all the employers, host families, nannies and au pairs who completed our lengthy survey and whose contributions have underpinned the content of the book. Special thanks to Christine Turner, who dedicated her evenings and weekends to enter all of the data into the computer for us.

Our appreciation also goes to all those people who gave us invaluable advice and help on the content of the book. Our particular thanks to Janet White of the Janet White Nanny Agency in Leeds, Renate Jones of Wimbledon Nannies, Julie Skinner of 'Special People' and Tricia Pritchard of the Professional Association of Nursery Nurses, who all provided us with expert advice and support on nanny-related issues. Thanks also to Tony Reiss and Tara Renton for advice on employing nannies with children; to Sarah Ingram for her ideas and helpful materials; and to Catharine Kesley for her advice about au pairs.

Our thanks go to Cecilia Burnette for her help in typing the book and to our agent, Teresa Chris, for believing in the book in the first place. Our great appreciation also to Helen Gummer, our editor, for her relaxed approach and unfailing encouragement and to Katharine Young for her support in seeing it through.

We are grateful to the children who attended our discussion groups and who contributed the delightful drawings and quotations that you see throughout the book: Wilfred and Felix Aylett, Alice Bacon, Bethany and Dominic Clarke, Brendan, Timothy and Rosie Gillott, Jamie and Daniel House, Matthew and Helen Ingram, Nicola Raeside and Toby Rickards.

Our appreciation also goes to those who took the time to review our text and to offer intelligent, helpful input and welcome encouragement: Jackie Clarke, Donna Franklin, Shelagh and Tony Turfrey, Iain Wightwick and Deborah Williams.

Thanks to our nannies, past and present, for their sterling efforts, affection, expertise and for the inspiration and learning that they've given us over the years: Emma Bohin, Sharon Boyles, Jackie Eyre, Lynsey Firth, Shelley Hepworth, Tara Jackson, Hilary Jones, Alex McCracken, Rachel Skidmore and Rebecca Spence.

Finally, thanks to our husbands and to our children. To Crispin, for his support and his precision proofreading. To Richard, for his technical help and his encouragement and enthusiasm. Both men were incredibly patient and did more than their fair share of child care while we were writing the book. And to Wilfred, Felix, Olivia, Elspeth, Jamie, Daniel and Edward, who enthusiastically supported us throughout – and without whom the book would not be.

Introduction

WHY THIS BOOK?

Times have changed. Nowadays many people want to enlist help to look after their children. Whether they go out to work or need some extra help at home, the person they choose and the way the arrangement works will affect their whole family.

We are working mothers ourselves. Our jobs involve training others to recruit and manage people. We believe that finding and managing a nanny or au pair requires a similar approach to that of the workplace. When it is done well, it can be a positive and enriching experience for everyone involved (parents, children and the nanny or au pair).

Of course, there have been occasions when we have not handled situations as well as we might have done and we've tried to learn from them. We have written this book to share our experiences and to help you to manage your own child-care arrangements with confidence. We hope that you'll find having a nanny or au pair as enjoyable and rewarding as we have.

WHAT DOES THE BOOK AIM TO DO?

For many of us the prospect of recruiting and managing our own nanny or au pair can make us feel ill at ease. It can be hard to feel rational when we are making decisions which affect our children. We might also be stepping into unfamiliar territory when we employ someone in our own home, and feel uncertain of the right way to do things.

Our book provides practical advice and guidance to help you to deal with just about any situation you might have to face. In some cases there are no right or wrong answers – so we provide you with options and alternatives to consider.

We have given guidance on many of the questions that we have often pondered ourselves.

- Should I use a nursery, or employ a nanny or an au pair?
- Where do I find a nanny or au pair?
- How do I know how much to pay her? What do I do about paying tax and national insurance? When should I increase her pay?
- I'm interviewing some nannies or au pairs tomorrow, what questions should I ask?
- Our new au pair joins us next week. What do we need to do to prepare?
- My nanny is great with the children but very untidy. I don't want to upset her but it is hard to come back to an untidy house at the end of the day. What should I do?
- My nanny keeps going off sick. How should I handle it?
- My au pair is homesick. How do I help her but let her know at the same time that it's affecting us all?
- Our nanny or au pair leaves next week. The children love her. How do we ensure that her departure is a happy one?

As part of our research we sent a detailed survey to nannies, their employers, au pairs and their host families. We received two hundred and seventy responses from across the country and the results of the survey are included and explained throughout the book.

Any advice on the subject of nannies and au pairs which ignores the opinions of children does so at its peril. With this in mind, we canvassed the views of children through a number of interactive discussions (our admiration for the teaching profession has increased tenfold since the experience). The children made an important contribution. Their pictures, drawn during our discussions with them, are reproduced with their permission throughout the book.

The book is divided into four stages. Within each chapter you will find helpful guidelines, examples and 'how to' descriptions. We have also included short case studies based on situations which we have experienced ourselves, or which were described in the survey. At the end of each chapter is a summary, which recaps the key points made during that chapter.

THE STAGES IN THE LIFE CYCLE OF A NANNY AND AU PAIR

I

Finding your nanny or au pair

Child-care options; identifying your requirements and deciding who to interview; interviewing and selecting; the final stages of recruitment

II

Managing the relationship

Setting the relationship up for success; communicating; managing and motivating your nanny or au pair; setting the terms and conditions (pay, pocket money, hours and benefits)

III

Managing problems, boundaries and specific situations

Handling issues, crises and gross misconduct; managing the boundaries

IV

Managing your changing needs

Handling child care as your needs change; ensuring happy endings

Employing a nanny and hosting an au pair are two very different challenges. Throughout the book, we have referred to nannies, mentioning au pairs when the comments also apply to them or referring to them separately when they are distinctly different.

NB. We have referred to all nannies and au pairs as 'she' for the sake of convenience. Male nannies and au pairs do exist, although unfortunately they are a relatively rare phenomenon. When we refer to parents and host families, we obviously include fathers as well as mothers. In some places, we have referred to 'mothers' alone; however, we recognise that it may be the father who is mainly or solely responsible for recruiting and managing the nanny or au pair.

ABOUT US

We are two working mothers who have employed nannies for many years. Between us we have employed live-in and live-out nannies and we have both taken part in nanny-share arrangements. One of us lives in London and the other in Yorkshire, so we are well aware of the regional variations involved in employing a nanny or hosting an au pair.

OUR BELIEFS AND VALUES

Our recommendations about how to manage nannies and au pairs are underpinned by our own beliefs and values about how they should be treated. You may find that you agree with us, or you may have different views in some areas. Whatever your position, it is helpful to have thought it through and we provide our ideas as a prompt for your own thoughts.

- Being a nanny or an au pair is a difficult role for relatively low pay. How would we feel about doing it? We should be realistic about what we expect her to achieve, given the nature of the role.
- We are not perfect, so it is unfair to expect our child carer to be.
- We should respect our nanny or au pair and treat her as we ourselves would like to be treated at work or by a family we were staying with.

- The most important part of a nanny's role is to look after the children and make sure they are safe and happy. All else is secondary. We should be reasonable with our requests.
- It is vital to form a good relationship and communicate often with our nanny or au pair. This includes establishing clear boundaries for the relationship.
- Everyone responds well to praise and we should always recognise our nanny's or au pair's efforts.
- We all make mistakes, and we should acknowledge and learn from them.
- Generally speaking, you get what you pay for. It is short-sighted to pay your child carer less than the going rate and expect her to do a good job.

We hope that you find the book helpful, informative and enjoyable.

Part I:

Finding Your Nanny or Au Pair

1 Child Care: What Are Your Options?

'Some of my colleagues at work advised me to use a nursery; others said to have a nanny. Everyone seemed to have strong views. In the end I had to decide what would suit our circumstances the best. The nanny won.' – *Mum*

When you are faced for the first time with a decision about child care, the options can be confusing. What you decide will depend on where you want your children to be cared for, the hours of cover required, and how much you can afford to pay. In this chapter, we outline the main child-care options and some of the advantages and disadvantages of each.

NANNIES

A nanny is someone aged eighteen or above, usually female, who you employ to look after your children in your own home.

Nannies can live in your home or live in their own homes and travel to you daily (see the tables on pp. 10 and 11 for the advantages and disadvantages of each option). Unlike other forms of child care, there is as yet no register of approved nannies and they are not subject to any checks by social services unless they work for more than two families at one time. Anyone can call herself a nanny although there are several qualifications which are relevant (see Chapter 2 for a summary). Nannies often distinguish themselves from au pairs and mother's helps by virtue of this professional training. Most nannies consider their job to be looking after the children in all respects (caring, playing, washing and ironing their clothes, cooking and cleaning up after the children) but not doing other housework or general domestic duties.

Nannies are not subject to legal restrictions on how many hours a week they can work. It is up to you to decide what it is you need – and what you can reasonably ask her to do.

Live-in nannies normally work up to fifty-five hours a week, that is, five eleven-hour days. They may also be expected to do up

LIVE-IN NANNIES

Advantages	Disadvantages
The nanny becomes a part of your family and the children get to know her really well, very quickly.	She will need to be provided with her own room/rooms.
She is on call whenever you need her (within your agreed hours). Punctuality is less likely to be an issue.	Everyone loses a bit of privacy.
She might be able to help with baby-sitting at short notice.	You may become more involved in her personal life and, potentially, personal problems.
She may be able to continue to care for the children when she is feeling a little unwell.	There will inevitably be an increase in your domestic costs – food, telephone, electricity, etc.
You pay less in terms of salary.	You may become more aware of and perhaps irritated by each other's personal habits – the relationships are more intense.
She may feel more tied to you as you provide her home as well as her job – and she may give you more notice when she leaves.	She may not stay as long because she may leave you to become more independent.
She can provide 24-hour care if/when necessary.	

to two baby-sitting sessions on top of this (during the week). A live-out nanny often works around forty-five to fifty hours a week, that is, five nine- or ten-hour days. Live-out nannies may be willing to baby-sit once or twice a week for extra pay but may well have other commitments in the evenings. Some nannies work longer hours than this; see Chapter 8 for details.

All nannies normally expect two days off a week. A nanny will sometimes be happy to work a regular Saturday or Sunday, providing she has a corresponding day off in the week. Occasional weekend work may also be acceptable to her, providing you pay her well or give her plenty of time off in lieu. Finding a nanny who is prepared to work weekends as a regular commitment may be difficult.

How much you pay your nanny depends on her age and experience, her qualifications, where you live in the country and the hours you need her for. Nannies who live in are generally paid less than those who live out, because you provide their accommodation and food.

LIVE-OUT NANNIES

Advantages	Disadvantages
The nanny doesn't need accommodating in your home.	Your nanny will be less available to help at night/with baby-sitting etc.
Your family and the nanny retain their privacy.	You will have less control over sick leave – and your nanny may be off sick more often.
Everyone has a break at the end of the day.	Punctuality could be more of an issue.
There is less involvement in each other's personal lives/problems.	You will pay a higher salary.
There is no risk of your nanny feeling homesick.	24-hour cover may be more complex to arrange.

NANNY-SHARE ARRANGEMENTS

This is when two families agree to share a nanny's time. Their children may be cared for at the same time by the nanny, or they may split the week between them and each employ her on different days. One family usually pays the nanny and sorts out her tax and National Insurance. Arrangements for sharing the costs take into account the number of children cared for from each family, where the nanny and the children spend their time and the number of hours worked for each family. It can be a little complex to set up,

NANNY SHARES

Advantages

It reduces the cost of employing a nanny.

It may mean that the children are with other children through the day, which may help to develop their social skills.

You share the workload of employing someone (tax, National Insurance arrangements, etc.).

There is more chance of one of you being able to cover in the event of the nanny being ill – four parents to choose from, rather than two.

There is someone else to talk to about any problems or difficulties with your nanny – and someone else to be there with you when you try to sort them out.

Disadvantages

The arrangements need to be carefully agreed in advance so that each family feels the agreement is fair. If not, it is easy for resentment to build up.

Both families need to reach agreement on basic issues such as discipline and food, so that the nanny can be consistent in her treatment of the children.

Sometimes one family is happier than the other with the nanny's performance and she can become de-motivated as a result.

The nanny may prefer one family or child to the other.

but there are clear advantages if you can find another family and a nanny willing to take part.

If a nanny looks after children from more than two families in the same place and at the same time, she must be registered by the local authority.

More information about nanny-share arrangements can be found in Chapters 4, 8, 10 and 12.

AU PAIRS

Au pairs are not usually trained to look after children. They are young, unmarried people (usually female) from the following countries outside the European Union.

Andorra	Macedonia
Bosnia-Herzegovina	Malta
Croatia	Monaco
Cyprus	San Marino
Czech Republic	Slovakia
Faroe Islands	Slovenia
Greenland	Switzerland
Hungary	Turkey

The Home Office guidelines say that au pairs must be single, aged between seventeen and twenty-seven, with no dependants. They come to this country for the experience of living with a British family and to learn English and they should be allowed time to attend English-language classes. Au pairs from some countries must obtain a visa before travelling to the UK and some must register with the police within seven days of arriving in the country (your au pair agency will advise you about this, or you can find the information on the Home Office website; see Useful Contacts at the end of the book).

The Home Office is quite clear about how much work an au pair should do. They may work for up to five hours each day and a maximum of twenty-five hours each week (with two full days off) in return for pocket money, board and lodging. Additionally, they are allowed to baby-sit up to twice a week. Their tasks involve caring for your children and helping with a variety of light jobs around the home. They live with you as a family member – 'au pair' means 'as a peer' or 'equal'. The term 'host family' is used to describe 'employers' of au pairs.

Au pairs are not employees and should not be expected to have sole care of babies and young children under three.

Most au pairs stay with a family for between six months and one year. Au pairs may only stay in the UK for a maximum of two years.

The availability of au pairs varies throughout the year. There tends to be an influx of au pairs into the UK in September and to a lesser extent in January, and they tend to work until June or July. Another group of au pairs come to the UK to work over the summer (May to August).

One wise lady who has hosted several au pairs said, 'Understand that these are young girls – still teenagers some of them – who have little experience of running a home or managing children. It's best not to expect too much – then you might be pleasantly surprised!'

European Community 'au pairs'

Strictly speaking, the term 'au pair' applies only to people from the countries listed above. In practice, however, it is also used to describe other Europeans from the EU who come over to learn English and who want to stay with a family and earn some pocket money. In this case there are no Home Office guidelines. Agencies usually recommend that they work similar hours.

Au pair plus

This term applies to au pairs from EU countries only, who may work for a greater number of hours each week for more pocket money.

If you and your au pair both agree to this type of arrangement, agencies usually recommend up to a maximum of thirty-eight hours a week, plus up to two nights baby-sitting. Au pairs should still be allowed to attend language classes during the daytime and should be allowed at least one full day off a week.

Some agencies do not recognise the concept of au pair plus, as there is evidence of young people being exploited under this type of arrangement. For example, some host families see it as a means of obtaining a cheap housekeeper or mother's help.

MOTHER'S HELPS

This is the other major child-care option if you wish to have your child looked after in your own home. Mother's helps are usually not formally trained in child care, although they may well have plenty of experience of children, perhaps their own. They expect to do some light housework and other domestic duties as well as helping to look after your children. They are *not* domestic cleaners. Some mother's helps live in and others visit daily. Their hours are often similar to those of nannies.

Like nannies and au pairs, mother's helps are not registered and are not subject to local authority checks.

Nanny agencies can often help you to find a mother's help, or you can advertise in the local press (see Chapter 2 for more information).

To help you to decide which option will suit you best, see the table below.

NANNIES, AU PAIRS AND MOTHER'S HELPS

NANNIES

Particularly suitable when you need flexible/long hours of sole care

Advantages	Disadvantages
They can provide your child with constant, individual care on a full-time basis.	Nannies do not always stay as long as you want them to, so continuity of care may be an issue.

Advantages	Disadvantages
Being based in your own home provides a secure, familiar environment for your child.	Your domestic bills will be higher, as the house is occupied during the day.
Your children do not have to be dressed and taken out early in the morning or late at night.	It may be a more expensive option, particularly if you have only one child.
You can design your nanny's hours and job to suit your particular requirements.	You may have to provide your nanny with her own car.
You can manage the environment in which your child is cared for and make your own rules.	You may not want to have visits by her friends during the day (or night!).
With more than one child it can be a cost-effective form of child care.	

AU PAIRS

Particularly suitable when you are at home and need part-time help with the children and with general household duties

Advantages	Disadvantages
They provide a flexible helping hand for child care and light household duties.	An au pair is not appropriate if you need someone to have sole care of younger children.
They can be a useful baby-sitting resource.	Language difficulties may make it difficult to communicate with your au pair and for her to create a rapport with you and your children.
You can design the hours your au pair helps (maximum of five hours a day) to suit your own routine.	She will probably not be able to help with your child's development in the same way that an English-speaking, qualified nanny can.

Advantages	Disadvantages
They are an inexpensive form of additional help – au pairs are paid 'pocket money' in return for board and the experience of living with an English family.	Most au pairs stay for only 6–12 months, so there will be little continuity of care. You may need to provide significant help or guidance on how to do jobs. You are supposed to treat her as one of the family, so she may well encroach on your personal time with your partner and children.

MOTHER'S HELPS

Particularly suitable if you need help around the home and with the children.

Advantages	Disadvantages
They provide a flexible helping hand for child care and light household duties (e.g., shopping, laundry). It can be a flexible option when your children are at school and you don't need full-time help. You can design the hours your mother's help works, to suit your own routine.	It is more expensive than hosting an au pair. A mother's help often costs a little less than a nanny but is usually less qualified. She may not be suitable to provide sole care of a child (particularly pre-school).

MATERNITY NURSES

Maternity nurses are usually employed to help you just before and immediately after you have a baby – although occasionally people keep them on for years. They are highly trained (they are often qualified nannies with several years' experience of caring for babies). Maternity nurses usually live in with the family. They are an expensive option, costing more than a qualified nanny. However, they can be a great help, particularly with a first baby. They help with all aspects of caring for the baby, including getting up during the night. However, you may prefer to care for the baby yourself and have additional help with the housework. If so, a temporary mother's help or a cleaner or housekeeper will be more appropriate.

Finding a maternity nurse can be difficult. They are often in short supply and have to be booked well in advance of the birth of your baby. As the birth is not usually predictable, this can make life quite complicated and you may have to pay a stand-by fee. Unless you know of any maternity nurses yourself, an agency is probably the best way to get hold of one.

Doulas

Whereas the focus of the maternity nurse is on the baby, a doula's main emphasis is on looking after you, just before, during or just after the birth of your baby. Her role is to keep balance and harmony in your home while you focus your attention on your new baby. She helps to look after any other children, assists around the home and provides you with support, guidance and practical help. She may or may not have a relevant qualification, but she will be an experienced mother herself. Working full- or part-time, she will usually be with you for a defined period (one to three months) after the birth of your baby. Like maternity nurses, doulas tend to be an expensive option.

Certain agencies will be able to supply you with details of doulas in your area. Alternatively, some doulas advertise directly in local papers and magazines.

As maternity nurses and doulas usually focus on the first few weeks of a baby's life, we have not considered them as a long-term child-care option.

WHEN YOU NEED MORE HELP IN YOUR HOME

A small minority of families may feel that one nanny or au pair is not sufficient to meet all their child-care needs. This can happen when there is a child with special needs, for example, or when the family is particularly large or busy. Sometimes people need additional cover for a short period, for example while recuperating from an operation, after the birth of a baby, or when moving house.

In these circumstances, you need to decide which combination of child care will be most appropriate. You could combine a nanny and an au pair, for example, to provide you with more cover over the weekends. Or you could employ a housekeeper so that your nanny doesn't have to do any nursery duties.

If you do need to employ more than one person, there will almost certainly be relationship and boundary issues to consider. They are covered in detail in Chapter 11.

OTHER CHILD-CARE OPTIONS OUTSIDE YOUR HOME

Child minders (for children of all ages)

Child minders are individuals who look after your children, usually in their own home. They have to be registered, which involves meeting certain criteria relating to safety and comfort, and they are subject to annual random checks by social services. They normally look after other children as well as your own and are usually a cheaper option than employing a nanny or using a private day nursery. The hours they are willing to work vary. Contact your local authority for more information and for a list of registered child minders in your area.

Nursery classes and nursery schools (for three- to five-year-olds)

They are run along school lines and are usually open during termtime from 9 am to 3.30 pm. They are often free (when run by the local authority) and may be attached to a primary school. Other nursery schools are private and fee-paying. They all have to be registered and are inspected regularly.

Day nurseries (for babies, from six weeks old, to five-year-old children)

They open for longer hours than nursery classes and schools, and aim to provide all-day care. Some offer after-school clubs and holiday clubs for older children. They are registered by the local authority and inspected regularly. There are three types of day nursery.

Community and council nurseries
These are usually free but offer places first to families with a particular need, for example, where there is only one parent, who has to work. Some offer fee-paying places to other families.

Private nurseries
They are set up as small businesses and are fee-paying. Prices vary, so shop around.

Workplace nurseries
Some enlightened employers run excellent nurseries for the children of their employees.

Pre-schools (for three- to five-year-olds)
They are set up by parents and provide sessions of play and education for pre-school-age children. Each child can usually attend for two to five sessions a week and a minimal charge is made. They may not be available in your area (although you could always set one up). The local authority inspects them regularly.

Local authorities are required to publish regular reports about child minders, nurseries and pre-schools. The information is available to parents. Try your social services department or local library for copies.

QUESTIONS TO HELP YOU DECIDE WHICH OPTION TO CHOOSE

Which child-care option suits you best will depend on a number of factors. We have drawn up a list of questions to help you to consider the issues.

1 Do I want my child to be looked after in my home or in a nursery environment?
2 Which option will be most convenient – having someone come to the house or dropping the children off?
3 How old are my children and which option is best suited to them?
4 What hours do I need care for? Are these hours longer than a nursery or child minder can provide? Am I ever late and, if so, by how much and how often? What will I do during school holidays?
5 Will one solution meet my needs, or should I be thinking about multiple child-care assistance?
6 Do I want my child to be brought up with lots of other children or not?
7 How important is continuity of care to me? (Nurseries guarantee continuity of location, but carers may change more frequently. Most au pairs stay for a year or less. Nannies may stay longer. In our survey 26 per cent of nannies had been with their current family for more than two years and 28 per cent for between one and two years.)
8 What will happen when my child is ill? (Nurseries and child minders can't usually take ill children, whereas a nanny or au pair can. On the other hand, when you employ a nanny you are dependent on her good health and you are vulnerable if she is ill, which doesn't happen with a nursery.)
9 How much can I afford to pay? (Employing a nanny becomes more cost-effective the more children you have. If you do choose to employ a nanny, don't forget the additional costs such as electricity, gas, food, petrol and telephone bills.)

SUMMARY

- There are many options to consider when deciding the form of child-care assistance you need.
- Nannies, au pairs and mother's helps are all based in your home.
- Child minders, nursery classes/schools, day nurseries and pre-schools all involve out-of-home care, usually with other children.
- Our book is written for parents who want help in their own home, in the form of a nanny or an au pair (although much of what we say applies to mother's helps, too).

2 Identifying Your Requirements and Deciding Who to Interview

'We like her because she does what we want to and not the housework.' – Child

'Be clear in your own mind what sort of person you want, for what purpose – and don't compromise.' – Mum

Every family has different needs and different preferences. An excellent nanny in one home might be considered mediocre in another. That is why agencies cannot do the whole job for you. So, whether you enlist the help of others – or plan to recruit someone on your own – you need to think carefully about the type of person you are looking for.

CLARIFYING WHAT THE ROLE ENTAILS

Your first task is to think carefully about what you will want your nanny or au pair to do. It is important that you define your requirements carefully at this stage, as the rest of your recruitment will be based upon them.

The following list outlines the things that most people would expect their nanny to do. An au pair might be expected to help you with these tasks, although she might also help with general household chores or light housework, such as doing the laundry or vacuum cleaning.

- Look after, entertain and help to develop your child.
- Wash and iron your child's clothes.
- Keep your child's room, toys and wardrobe clean and tidy.
- Cook meals for your child.
- Keep the house as she finds it: tidy up after herself and the children – but not after you.

However there is room for interpretation in this list and you need to decide what is important to you. Some families insist that the children are taken swimming regularly, for example. What do you want your nanny to do with your child? Don't just list what you would do yourself if you were at home. One of the advantages of a nanny, and to a lesser extent of an au pair, is that she can bring a range of skills you don't have and which your children can benefit from.

The table below shows some of the activities you might ask your nanny to carry out. You may prefer to carry out some of them yourself or to add others, but it gives an idea of your choices. Some items are also relevant for au pairs.

ACTIVITIES A NANNY MAY BE ASKED TO CARRY OUT

Caring activities

Cooking for your child (mixed, balanced diet).

Dressing your child/choosing his/her clothes.

General hygiene/care (washing, changing nappies, cleaning teeth, etc.).

Taking your child to the doctor, dentist or clinic.

Taking your child to and from school/nursery or other activities.

Caring activities

Managing bathtime and bedtime effectively.

'Proxy parenting': looking after your child during the night/ 24-hour care.

Looking after your child when he or she feels unwell.

Child-centred activities

Art and craft work (painting, sticking, making cards, play dough etc.).

Swimming.

Taking your child on trips out (museums, parks, local attractions, play areas, etc.).

Attending toddler groups and playgroups.

Cooking/baking (with your child).

Singing, musical play, nursery rhymes.

General play ('let's pretend' games, board games, jigsaws, making dens, playing with toys).

Helping with homework/reading practice.

Assisting your child's intellectual development (e.g., speech, reading, writing, drawing, visits to the library, helping on the computer).

Assisting your child's physical development (e.g., sitting, walking, potty training, riding a bike, skipping).

Accompanying the family on outings or on holiday.

Household management activities

Washing and ironing your child's clothes.

Cleaning toys, rooms, wardrobes and drawers.

Tidying the areas the child uses in the house.

Sewing your child's clothes (e.g., buttons, school name labels).

Packing your child's case for weekends away and for holidays.

Note: Children with special needs may have additional requirements.

Once you have decided what you want your nanny or au pair to do, you can start to write a simple job description (or, for an au pair, a list of activities). From this, you will be able to decide what questions to ask during the interview.

Writing a job description

In putting together a job description it is important to make the responsibilities clear – without putting in so much detail that your nanny feels overwhelmed and over-controlled. We came upon one nanny whose job description extended to eighteen pages. Needless to say, she felt that she wasn't given the freedom she wanted to use her professional judgement and skill.

Generally speaking one to two pages is sufficient. Key areas to cover include the main areas of responsibility, together with any rules which are important to you.

Formal job descriptions are not appropriate for au pairs, as they are not employees. However, in our survey just over half the host families who responded did provide their au pair with a written summary of the main tasks she would be asked to help with.

EXAMPLE JOB DESCRIPTION FOR A LIVE-OUT NANNY

Job description for [name of nanny], nanny for [names of children]

The purpose of your job

To ensure that the children are safe and happy. To create a positive and stimulating environment, so that the children develop effectively.

Key responsibilities

- To ensure that the children are kept warm, comfortable and clean.
- To provide a balanced diet for the children.
- To follow the normal daily routine (school and nursery runs, etc.) in a cheerful and happy manner, so that you and the children have as much fun as possible. This will include taking them on excursions and doing a variety of activities each day (e.g., reading, drawing, painting, singing, swimming, walking, visiting the library).
- To stimulate, play with and entertain the children so that they are continually learning and are happy and content.

- To wash and iron the children's clothes and keep their rooms, toys and cupboards tidy and clean.
- To assist with household duties related to the children, ensuring as a minimum that the house is left tidy at the end of the day.
- To arrange interesting and fun activities for all the children during the school holidays.

Note: The job description is not the same as the contract of employment, which formally lays out the details of employment (hours, pay, holidays, etc.).

Sometimes families choose to include the 'house rules' in the job description. A suggested list of house rules is given in Chapter 5.

IDENTIFYING THE SORT OF PERSON YOU NEED

Once you have decided what you want your nanny or au pair to do, you need to decide what type of person you are looking for. Is a loving and affectionate person more important than someone who is highly organised and efficient, or are both equally important?

In our survey we asked employers and host families to prioritise the qualities they found most important in a nanny and an au pair. Their most common responses are shown in the table on p. 28. Unsurprisingly, perhaps, for both nannies and au pairs 'a love of children' was quoted three times more frequently than any of the others.

It is worth making sure that you consider your medium-term child-care needs as well as your immediate ones. Some nannies may be excellent with small babies, for example, but at a bit of a loss with a two-year-old in a full-blown tantrum.

Similarly, it is worth considering what age of nanny you feel comfortable with. It is hard to generalise, but some employers feel happier with a younger nanny who they feel more able to train to suit their requirements. Others prefer older, more experienced nannies who may be more confident and knowledgeable.

Another area to consider is your own personal style. Are you likely to be quite directive and therefore need a nanny or au pair

THE MOST IMPORTANT QUALITIES OF A NANNY AND AN AU PAIR ACCORDING TO OUR SURVEY

(in order of importance)

Nanny	Au pair
1 Genuine love of/for the children	1 Love of children, enjoys their company
2 Honest, trustworthy, demonstrates integrity	2 Dependable, reliable
3 Dependable, reliable	3 Will help with and is good at housework
4 Practical, uses common sense, organised	4 Open, honest, trustworthy
5 Is fun, energetic	5 Flexible and adaptable
6 Flexible and adaptable	6 Reasonable command of English

who is generally happy to be told what to do? Or is your style to delegate more, and do you therefore need someone who has plenty of initiative and is willing to make her own decisions?

Here are some qualities you may look for in a nanny or an au pair. Select those which are important to you – remembering that with an au pair you may need to be a little less ambitious. Your preferences will help you to brief the agency about your requirements (if you decide to use one) and focus your questions during the interview.

QUALITIES YOU MAY NEED IN YOUR NANNY OR AU PAIR

Caring and affectionate. Quickly establishes rapport with the children.

Plenty of initiative/uses common sense.

Planning and organising skills.

Punctual, conscientious and healthy.

Able to develop the children and carry out a wide variety of activities.

Able to have fun: sparky and energetic.

Assertive: will manage discipline well and stand up for your children when necessary.

Calm in a crisis. Even-tempered.

Competent in a medical emergency.

Flexible.

Clean and tidy, well-presented personally.

Able to plan and cook a well-balanced diet. Sensible attitude to eating.

Enjoys physical activity: swimming, walking, etc.

Relates well to adults; not too shy or too dominant. Able to raise difficult issues.

Drives; has a clean driving licence.

Specific experience required (e.g., experience of babies/has looked after four children before).

Specific qualifications required (e.g., for nannies, CACHE, BTEC, NVQ).

Other items can be added. It may be essential to you that your nanny or au pair is a non-smoker, for example.

It is important that you think through this list of qualities and consider it carefully, as it will form the basis of the questions you ask, and the decisions you make, during your interviews.

Special needs

Children or families with special needs may well have additional requirements of their nanny, for example:

- Particular experience (and possibly qualifications) in the field in question (e.g., autism or deafness).
- Resilience. The family situation can be more complex and sensitive. Emotions may be more fraught on all sides.
- Physical strength may be required for some jobs. It might be important to have experience of lifting older children safely, for example.
- Sensitivity to the additional hazards and risks for the child, both within and outside the home.
- Motivation to work with that family/child and to learn about and respond to the condition/situation.
- Driving is usually essential.

Child-care Qualifications

Changes are made to child-care qualifications all the time. If you are unsure, it is best to check with the relevant awarding body (see Useful Contacts at the end of the book). Some of the main qualifications and awarding bodies are:

National Vocational Qualifications (NVQ) and Scottish Vocational Qualifications (SVQ)
In Early Years Care and Education

NVQs are awarded for competence in work situations, so they are highly practical qualifications. Different levels of NVQ reflect different degrees of competence; the levels you are most likely to come across are 2 and 3. The Professional Association of Nursery

Nurses accepts level 3 of the above NVQ as a suitable qualifier for membership.

The Council for Awards in Children's Care and Education (CACHE) Diploma in Childcare and Education (previously known as the Diploma in Nursery Nursing or the NNEB)
This is the traditional and best-known 'nanny' qualification. It is a full time, two-year course but it can be studied for on a part-time basis too. It is equivalent to NVQ level 3. There is a heavy practical emphasis to the course.

The Business and Technical Council (BTEC)
National Certificate or Diploma in Early Years previously known as the National Certificate or Diploma in Childhood Studies (Nursery Nursing)
The certificate is studied on a part-time basis, and the diploma on a full-time basis. Students are at least sixteen years old and usually need a minimum of four GCSEs at grade C or above (or equivalent). The courses are equivalent to NVQ level 3, and both have a high practical content.

The National Association for Maternal and Child Welfare (NAMCW)
It used to offer a one-year, full-time Advanced Level Certificate in Childcare and Education (equivalent to the knowledge requirements of NVQ level 2), and a two-year, full-time Diploma in Nursery Nursing (equivalent to NVQ level 3). Both courses had a high practical content. The NAMCW has now merged with CACHE.

Montessori Centre International
A specialist college offering child care/education training, based on the education philosophy of Maria Montessori and offering a variety of courses. Its Early Childhood Teaching Course and Nursery Foundation Teaching Course are equivalent to the knowledge requirements of an NVQ level 3.

The Chiltern College, Norland College and Princess Christian College
These are the three best-known residential colleges, providing training in early-years care. Each offers its own certificate in

addition to students attaining the CACHE Diploma in Childcare and Education and, in some cases, NVQ level 3.

City and Guilds

There are a number of City and Guilds courses relating to childcare, and each are now linked to an NVQ level. You should check whether the content of a particular course is suitable for your requirements.

For further information, contact the relevant organisation (the telephone numbers are given in Useful Contacts at the end of the book).

KNOWING WHERE TO FIND YOUR NANNY OR AU PAIR

The best ways to find a nanny or an au pair are to:

- Use an agency (really the best option for au pairs).
- Advertise in newsagents, shops, etc., and in magazines and newspapers.
- Use the internet. There are websites which allow you to advertise for a nanny or an au pair and/or to search a database of candidates. The service may be free (the provider making its money from advertising other companies on the website).

The grapevine can be a good source, too, but it is not a failsafe way of ensuring that you get the right person at the right time. Some employers approach nanny colleges and recruit directly from there. Alternatively, you could use a 'child-care consultancy'. These are organisations which help you through the process of recruitment. They often advertise in parenting magazines and local newspapers.

If you are interested in a nanny share, some agencies keep a register of families and nannies who are interested in such an arrangement. There are also nanny-share registers, set up by individuals. You pay a small fee to have your name and requirements placed on a list. Nanny-share registers are advertised in local newspapers and magazines, and some branches of the National Childbirth Trust (NCT) also have them (again, see Useful Contacts).

Whatever methods you use, it will probably take you around four weeks to find someone. After that, a nanny may have to give her current employer up to one month's notice. Au pairs who are already in this country may also have notice to give their host family and first time au pairs may have to apply for a visa before they can travel. In our survey 88 per cent of employers had managed to recruit their nanny within two months and 73 per cent had placed au pairs in the same period.

Using an agency

Anyone can set up a nanny or an au pair agency and, as yet, the industry is not regulated. However, most reputable agencies are members of the Recruitment and Employment Confederation (REC, formerly FRES), which has its own code of practice. Some au pair agencies are members of the International Au Pair Association (IAPA) instead, which also has a code of practice.

Advantages of using a good agency

- It saves you the time, expense and the bother of placing an advertisement and then answering calls or sifting through lots of letters and cvs.
- Agency staff are skilled at checking references and assessing nannies and au pairs – that is what they spend their whole time doing – so, while you must always check references yourself, it is encouraging to know that you have a double check built into the process.
- Agencies share information about unsuitable nannies and au pairs with one another.
- They should help you to deal with nanny- or au-pair-related problems or queries once you have chosen someone, and will advise on salaries, pocket money, hours of work, etc.
- They will find you someone else for minimal extra charge, should your nanny or au pair prove unsuitable (providing you

have paid their fees and let them know within an agreed time).
- They will help/advise you about the administration necessary when bringing an au pair into the country for the first time (letter of invitation, visa, police registration, etc.).

Disadvantages of using an agency
- It is more expensive than the other options (particularly if you live in London or the south of England, where agency fees tend to be significantly higher than the rest of the country).
- You are limited to the nannies or au pairs they have on their books at the time you apply. However, there is nothing to stop you from registering with more than one agency to increase your choice.

If you live in the south, you may well find that you have more choice of agencies than elsewhere in the country.

The fees charged by agencies vary significantly. There is often a small registration charge but most agencies only charge you the full amount if you choose a nanny or an au pair they have sent to you. Fees for nannies vary from a fixed amount to a proportion or percentage of the nanny's first year's salary. This may seem a lot, but don't forget that advertising can also be expensive and time-consuming. Fees for placing au pairs are usually less than for nannies, although most agencies have a variable rate: the longer the placement, the more you pay.

Questions to ask agency staff when deciding which agency to use
1. Are you a member of REC or IAPA? [If not, why not? Are their reasons good ones? How do they respond to the rest of the questions below?]
2. Where do you find your nannies/au pairs? What is your policy on recruiting/poaching nannies and au pairs already in position? [Don't use anyone who admits to poaching – it might be you they poach from next time!]
3. What is your agency fee and how is it calculated? At what point(s) do you charge?

4 How do you interview your nannies/au pairs? [For nannies it must be face to face.]
5 What type of references do you take? [They must be verbal as well as written. For au pairs, check whether they are child-care references or just general character references.]
6 How many references do you check? [It must be at least two before they refer someone to you.]
7 Can you send me a blank reference form? [Look at the questions they ask and compare them with the questions we suggest in Chapter 4.]
8 How many nannies/au pairs do you reject/refuse to have on your books?
9 What training have your staff received in interviewing?
10 What after-care services do you provide? [There should be some form of support/mediation in case of disputes between you and your nanny or au pair.]
11 What do you do if a nanny or au pair proves unsuitable? [There should be a guarantee/replacement service of some kind, and the guarantee period should be at least four weeks. Au pair agencies sometimes have accommodation which they can make available to au pairs should they have to leave a host family without another one to go to. If not, they will often assist with any arrangements that need to be made.]

A good agency will ask you for your requirements at the start of the process and will pre-select nannies/au pairs using those requirements. They will be able to advise you on salaries, pocket money (for au pairs), hours, benefits, and conditions of employment (for nannies). They may offer to come to see you in your home to help them to select the right person for you. Ask them to send you a copy of their terms and conditions of business and read them carefully before you proceed.

Agencies can be found in the Yellow Pages and many have their own websites. The REC and IAPA will provide you with their lists of approved nanny and au pair agencies (see our Useful Contacts).

Doing Your Own Advertising and Interviewing

Some people prefer to place an advertisement themselves and to take charge of the whole recruitment activity. This can be very effective and is usually cheaper than using an agency – but be prepared for it to take some time.

Receiving hundreds of responses from an advertisement is not what you are aiming for – in fact, it is often the sign of a poorly drafted advertisement, which is not sufficiently discriminating. Receiving a small number of applications from good-quality candidates is far preferable.

The steps are as follows:

1 Decide where to advertise. You can advertise free almost anywhere in your area: newsagents, shops, doctors' surgeries, schools, nurseries, etc. If you wish to spread your search further afield, *Nursery World* (a weekly magazine aimed at professionals involved in child care) or *The Lady* (another weekly magazine) may be used; you can also advertise in regional and local newspapers. If you are uncertain of the effectiveness of a particular publication, ring their advertising department and ask them about the size and nature of their readership. Ask them what days are best to advertise on and when adverts must be received in order to meet printing deadlines. If you are happy to employ a nanny straight out of college, you might also advertise at local colleges offering child-care qualifications.
2 Decide when to advertise. Make sure you are going to be around in the week after placing the advertisement, or that someone you can trust will be there to answer the telephone for you.
3 Draft your advertisement. Find examples of advertisements from the same paper/magazine. Look at the type of competition you will be facing from other advertisements. Yours needs to be at least average in its size and attractiveness in order to be successful. Some papers highlight the first few words of the advertisement in bold. If so, you will need to think carefully about the words you choose.

Include in your advertisement:

- The job title, e.g., 'full-time nanny'.
- The number and ages of the children involved.
- The location of the job.
- Any essential requirements, e.g., BTEC, driving licence, non-smoker.
- Some reference to pay, such as 'excellent pay' (putting the precise amount may limit your flexibility to negotiate later on).
- Any specific requirements, e.g., experience with special needs.
- Your telephone number, or instructions on how and when nannies can contact you. Some people prefer to ask for cvs to be sent to a box number. However, being able to speak to the applicants when they call you gives you a valuable opportunity to find out more about them at an early stage. We recommend that you speak to them first and ask them to send you their cv if they sound promising.
- NB. It is important to ensure that your advertisement is not discriminatory, e.g., by specifying an age limit.

Some employers ask their current nanny what she likes about the job and use that information to help them to design the advertisement. In the survey, we asked nannies what they would look for in their ideal job. The things that came top of the list were a good salary, a friendly, easy-going and likeable family, and having sole charge of the children. So if you want to make the job sound attractive, those are things you might want to mention.

Putting in a little about the family and the children will help to convey some of the family's personality and may well add to the appeal of the job. However, it is wise not to say too much, or to give the children's names or your address, for security reasons.

It is worth noting that most publications charge for each line of text, so keep it brief. Representatives will be able to quote you fees over the telephone, and newspapers usually accept the advertisement dictated to them. Some magazines may not.

SAMPLE JOB ADVERTISEMENT

Full-time nanny required to have sole charge of two boys aged 2 and 4 on a long-term basis in Leeds. We need a caring, fun-loving person who will work enthusiastically and flexibly. In return we offer excellent pay and benefits, with all weekends free. The job is non-residential and applicants must have their own car and be a non-smoker. A recognised child-care qualification is essential. Please telephone us on xxx xxxx after 7.30 pm for further details.

Using an internet search

Nannies and au pairs sometimes advertise directly on the internet and there are sites where you can place your own advertisement and/or look at the details of people wanting a job. There is obviously no vetting of these nannies or au pairs, so you do need to

THE INTERNET

Advantages	Disadvantages
Access to a wealth of applicants, not just those who are on agencies' books or who see your advertisement in the paper.	No screening of applicants (unlike an agency), and therefore more risky.
Cheaper than using an agency or advertising yourself.	More travel costs if applicants come for interviews from all over the country.
May be useful at certain times of the year when there are fewer nannies or au pairs around.	The number of cvs could be overwhelming.
Less pressure to recruit from a limited pool and take second best when you are pushed for time.	For an au pair, you will have to make all the arrangements for her entry into the UK and take full responsibility for her. You will also have to sort out the arrangements if the placement does not work out.

be careful. However, it may well be a useful source of information. It is worth doing a search to see what you can find.

As always, there are both pros and cons in using such a method.

Tips for using an internet search

- Be very specific when developing your criteria so you can focus on candidates who meet your brief.
- Follow up all references even more carefully than usual.
- For nannies, make sure you conduct at least one interview. If the person is coming a long way, making two interviews impracticable, ask her to spend a reasonable amount of time with you.
- Stipulate a probationary period so that you can cancel the arrangement if it does not work.
- Be careful about giving too many personal details in an advertisement that anyone can read.

DECIDING WHO TO INTERVIEW

When people respond to your advertisement or when you receive their details from the agency/internet, it is possible to do some pre-screening on the telephone, saving both you and the applicant time.

Make a list of all your essential requirements. For example, if it is vital that your nanny can drive, it is pointless interviewing anyone who can't. It is also important to tell the prospective nanny or au pair something about the job – the hours, location, the number, age and sex of your children – so that she can drop out if it doesn't appeal to her.

If you don't feel that the person is right for you, don't waste everyone's time by seeing her. However, be wary of jumping to conclusions at this stage. Better to end up doing one more interview than to miss the perfect person because her accent is too strong or because she seems too bossy on the telephone.

Ask nannies who meet your criteria to send you a copy of their cv (agencies usually do this for you). This is standard procedure – most qualified nannies will have one. Anyone who isn't really interested in the job is likely to drop out at this stage, saving you

TELEPHONE QUESTIONS TO PRE-SELECT NANNIES OR AU PAIRS FOR INTERVIEW

Useful questions	Comments
Name and telephone number.	Check that you have recorded the correct information so that you can easily contact her again.
Why are you interested in the position? What are your current circumstances, and why do you want to leave your current position?	This will give you useful information about whether she is currently employed or with a host family, and why she wishes to leave.
Why do you want to be a nanny/au pair?	Her response will give you an idea about what is important to her, and you can see if it matches your own views and values.
Ask any questions to which the answer is critical to you, e.g., have you got a professional qualification? Do you drive? Do you smoke? What experience do you have of looking after babies?	You need to decide these questions beforehand. Asking them will prevent you inviting inappropriate people to interview.
Tell me briefly about your experience of being a nanny/au pair. Or, for au pairs with no previous experience: Tell me briefly about your experience of looking after children.	We find this a useful question because during her response you can be listening for the things that are important to you, e.g., how articulate is she?

Useful questions	Comments
	How good is her English? How enthusiastic does she sound? Does she express warmth when talking about previous families and children?
What is your current pay? What salary are you expecting? (Not appropriate for au pairs).	Useful at this stage because it might rule out someone who is paid far more than you can afford. If you ask a few people, it will give you an idea of the going rate.
Where did you see the advertisement [if you placed it yourself]?	This gives you useful information about the success of your advertising, in case you have to find a nanny or au pair again in the future.

Note: A more comprehensive set of questions to ask au pairs, if you can't meet them in person, is given in Chapter 3.

more time. It will give you time to mull over their details and means that you don't have to decide there and then whether to invite them to interview. However, don't take too long. We once lost a nanny who sounded excellent, by taking too long at this stage.

Once the cvs and covering letters arrive, you can select who to interview. It is probably reasonable to expect to see three to six people. Ask all those invited to an interview to bring their references, certificates, driving license, and passport with them.

Finally, make sure that you call or write to everyone who sends you their cv – even if you aren't going to see them all – as this is common courtesy.

SUMMARY

- Decide what you want your nanny or au pair to do and write it down as a job description (for nannies) or a list of activities (for au pairs).
- Decide the type of person you are looking for, the qualities you need and any specific requirements (e.g., must be able to drive, mustn't smoke).
- Identify which methods you wish to use to recruit your nanny or au pair.
- Using an agency saves time. It is important to check that the agency is a reputable one. We have provided a list of questions you can ask the agency, which will enable you to do this. The agency will help you through the process and will give you valuable advice. For au pairs in particular, it is by far the best option; however, it is probably also the most expensive.
- Advertising locally or in magazines and/or newspapers keeps you in control of the process and means that you have access to a large number of applicants. However, it takes time, and there is no vetting of candidates so you need to be careful.
- Using the internet gives you access to many potential applicants and it may well be the cheapest option. However, there is no vetting of candidates so you need to be careful – and again, it could take a lot of time.
- If you are pre-selecting people yourself (from the internet or through other forms of advertising), it is important to vet people over the telephone before you decide who to interview. This saves you wasting valuable time interviewing unsuitable people.

3 Interviewing and Selecting Your Nanny or Au Pair

'Nannies are always nice to you when they're being interviewed.' – Child

'Always have two interviews – never make a rush decision.' – Mum

'It was difficult for me to talk to the mother because of my English.' – Au pair

'I don't think they got to know me – the interview was too formal.' – Nanny

Even though good agencies will interview for you, it is essential with both a nanny and an au pair to carry out your own interviews. In this chapter we provide lots of tips on how to interview, together with over a hundred interview questions for you to choose from.

While we recommend that you do interview au pairs, we believe that a different type of interview is appropriate. For many au pairs, just talking in English will be a challenge in itself – it is, after all, to improve their English that most of them come over here in the first place. Remember that au pairs are not employees but people you are taking into your family for a certain period of time. For all these reasons, your interview needs to be less formal and probably less challenging.

This chapter is written to help people to interview prospective nannies. However, bearing the above provisos in mind, many of the tips and questions will also be relevant to interviewing au pairs. In addition, we have provided a list of questions to ask when you need to interview your au pair over the telephone.

PREPARING FOR THE INTERVIEWS

Even if you decide to use an agency, it is a mistake to assume that they have done the interview for you and that you merely need to see if you like the nanny or au pair. The agency staff, no matter how good they are, do not live in your home and share your priorities and values. You need to conduct a thorough interview with all the people you see.

Issues to consider

- Try to have someone else present during the interview, as it will help you to make a more objective decision. It is a good idea for the nanny or au pair to meet all the family, so if appropriate involve your partner.
- Think about the timing of the interview. It is important for the nanny or au pair to meet the children so that you can observe how they relate to one another. However, don't forget that you are selling the job to her. If she is good, she may have other offers in the pipeline. It is not ideal to present three dirty, tired and squabbling children, ten minutes before bathtime. (If this is your only option – and we've been there ourselves – try to think of ways of limiting the damage.)
- Allow an hour to an hour and a half for each interview (two hours apart if you are running them consecutively).
- It is usual to offer your nanny or au pair interview expenses, particularly if she has travelled a long way to see you. So have some cash ready for her.
- Involve your children in the decision (if they are old enough) – and trust their judgement.

Deciding how much to pay/provide in benefits

You will have your own views on pay and benefits, which will depend in part on how much you can afford. Remember that rates differ significantly from one region to another and that a live-out nanny will expect to earn considerably more than a live-in nanny. Au pairs will expect a specific amount (recommended by the Home Office).

You need to think about all the following issues, as they are likely to be raised by the nannies or au pairs during the interview.

- How much will you pay and what other benefits will you offer (rooms for live-in nannies and au pairs, car, petrol, mobile phone, etc.)?
- How often will you increase your nanny's pay? (Not applicable to au pairs.)
- How much holiday will she have and when will she be able to take it – at any time, or when you take yours? What is your policy on working bank holidays?
- What is your policy on sick pay?
- What hours do you need and how/what will you pay for overtime?

Note: there is more detail and information on all of these areas in Chapters 8 and 9.

DECIDING WHAT QUESTIONS TO ASK

We are both used to interviewing people in our professional lives and yet, when it comes to interviewing nannies for our own children, we know how easy it is to lose courage. However, there are some basic guidelines, which really do help.

Things to check for in the cv

- Look at the dates. Unexplained gaps may be significant, so ensure you ask about them. They might mean that the nanny was sacked, for example.
- Look at the qualifications and hobbies/pastimes. What do they tell you about her interests and skills and what she will enjoy doing with your children?
- Look at the history of employment. How much experience has

she had, and what ages were the children? How similar have her jobs been to your job? What have been the main differences?

Asking questions about the qualities you are looking for

Research into interviewing techniques clearly shows that asking questions about each of the qualities you are looking for is a far more effective and reliable method of interviewing than the traditional 'tell me about yourself' approach that is commonly used.

Go back to your description of the sort of person you require and formulate questions around each of the qualities you are looking for. Make sure they are 'open' questions. Those that begin with words like 'how', 'what' and 'which' generally elicit more detailed responses than 'closed' questions – such as 'How old are you?' and 'Where do you live?' – which tend to encourage one-word responses. The latter are useful when you want a direct answer to a question like 'Do you smoke?', but they do not generally encourage people to talk or to share their views.

Try to avoid implying the answer you are looking for in the question itself. For example, it is far better to say, 'What aspects of being a nanny do you enjoy most?' than 'Do you like children?'

EXAMPLE QUESTIONS FOR INTERVIEWING A NANNY

It isn't intended that you ask all of these questions, but you can select from them and add your own as well. Some are appropriate for interviewing au pairs, although those interviews should generally be lower-key and less-challenging.

Starting the interview

Introduce yourself, your partner and the children (as appropriate).

Try to encourage the interviewee to relax. Make her a drink if she wants one.

If appropriate, show her round the house (or you may choose to do this later if you think she has interviewed well).

Starting the interview

Explain that you will be taking notes and that she should ask you any questions as you go.

Start by telling her a little more about the job.

Useful general questions

Why do you want to be a nanny? Why have you applied for this job?

Which parts of your current job do you enjoy most? Why?

Which parts do you enjoy least? Why? What was the worst bit about your last job? Why?

What are you most proud of having achieved in your current job/in your life in general?

What is the most difficult situation you have had to handle? What did you do? In hindsight what would you have done differently?

What do you see as your main strengths as a nanny?

What do you see as the main differences between a child minder and a nanny?

What are the areas where you are less strong/need to develop?

What do you look for in your employer?

What do you like to do in the evenings?

What would you like to do/achieve in the long term?

Are there any subjects on which you hold strong views, which might affect the way you perform your role as a nanny?

Note: If any of your children has special needs, you may have some additional questions.

Specific questions for each quality you want to assess

Caring and affectionate.

What do you feel are the three most important characteristics in a nanny?

Why did you want to be a nanny?

Specific questions for each quality you want to assess

Tell me how you felt/feel about leaving your last/current family?

Tell me about your own family.

How would you describe your own upbringing? What was good about it? What was not so good?

Note: Observe how she relates to the children.

Use of initiative.

Give me an example of a difficult situation you've been in with children. What did you do?

What lessons have you learnt in the last year about caring for children?

What suggestions have you made to your employer?

Planning and organising skills.

Describe how you have planned a day trip to [a local attraction].

Describe how you organise your day at the moment.

Describe a party you organised for the children. What worked well/less well? What would you do differently next time?

Punctual, conscientious and healthy.

How many days have you had off sick in the last year? Why?

What is your current state of health?

Have you had all the major childhood illnesses?

Are there any health issues which might affect the way you look after the children or your attendance at work?

Have you any special dietary requirements?

Do you smoke?

Note: If you have pets, check that she has no allergies to them.

Specific questions for each quality you want to assess

Able to develop the children and carry out with them a wide variety of activities appropriate to their ages.

Describe the development stages of the children you are looking after at the moment; *or*: Discuss the likely development needs of children aged [give your children's ages].

Describe what you might do in a typical day/week with my/our children.

How have you contributed to the development of the children you have looked after?

Able to have fun. Sparky and energetic.

Which aspects of looking after children do you enjoy most?

Which aspects of looking after children do you enjoy least? Why?

What type of thing makes you feel that you've had a bad day?

What are your outside interests?

Note: Observe her sense of humour, body language, tone of voice, facial expressions, enthusiasm when talking, and her general energy levels.

Assertive. Will manage discipline well and stand up for your children when necessary.

What are your views on discipline?

How far will you go when trying to discipline a child?

Tell me about a time when you had to deal with a tantrum. What did you do?

What is the most difficult disciplinary situation you have been in with children? What did you do?

Note: Observe her reactions to you and your questions during the interview. Is she reasonably assertive when you challenge her? Does she become defensive or aggressive?

Calm in a crisis; even-tempered.

When was the last time you felt angry/frustrated/upset at work? Why? What happened?

Specific questions for each quality you want to assess

What do you find the most frustrating thing about looking after children?

What is the most difficult situation you have had to deal with at work? What did you do? With hindsight, what might you have done differently?

When did you last lose your temper? What happened?

What makes you feel tired at work?

Tell me about an emergency you've been involved in. What happened? What did you do? With hindsight, what might you have done differently?

Have you any phobias/particular fears?

First-aid skills.

What would you do if a child fell over and bumped his head badly/burnt himself/cut his finger/started to choke/became feverish/became unusually drowsy/fell on his arm?

What are the symptoms of meningitis?

What safety hazards are you likely to find in the home/in this room?

What accidents have you had to cope with? What happened? What did you do?

Flexibility.

What is your view of the duties a nanny can be asked to do?

Have you ever been asked to do something you considered beyond the call of duty? What was it?

What is the longest day you have worked? How did you feel about it?

How do you feel about us being around occasionally/often?

How do you feel about the hours required in this job?

Tell me about any issues on which you have strong views.

Specific questions for each quality you want to assess

How would you feel about coming on holiday with the family?

How do you feel about looking after the children alone (this is sometimes called 'proxy parenting') for short periods (including nights) while we are both away? Have you ever done this? How long was it for? How did you feel about it? What were the pros and cons?

Clean and tidy; well-presented personally.

In your current job, what tidying do you do?

Tell me about the last time you sorted out the children's toys? How did you go about it?

Note: She will probably be at her smartest for the interview. Check that she is practically dressed – high shoes, glamorous clothes, swinging jewellery etc. are probably not appropriate.

Can cook; sensible attitude to eating.

What type of meals do you cook for the children you are looking after at the moment?

How do you plan their meals each week?

What do you do with the children while you prepare their evening meal?

What rules do you enforce at mealtimes?

Enjoys physical activity.

What physical exercise do you do with the children at the moment?

What do you do in your own spare time?

Relates well to adults – not too shy or too dominant, and can raise difficult issues.

How do you communicate with your existing employer? How would you alter/improve things if you could?

What was the last difference of opinion you had with your employer and how was it resolved?

Specific questions for each quality you want to assess

Who was the best boss/worst boss you have had in the past, and why?

Note: you can observe how well she relates to you during the interview.

Give details of the job's terms and conditions

Tell her the duties, hours, holidays, sick pay, perks, etc.

The issue of pay will need to be addressed. Ask her how much she is earning now and how much she expects. This gives you the opportunity to respond accordingly. Encourage her to consider the total package as well as the basic salary.

Tell her about any drawbacks or potential downsides of the job, e.g., 'I'm three months pregnant and I work from home two days a week.' Be honest and upfront about them.

Explain any rules you have which might affect her decision to take the job if it was offered (e.g., for a live-in nanny, rules about overnight guests).

Additional points

Has she applied for any other jobs? What stage is she at with her applications?

When would she be able to start?

How would she feel about overlapping with your current nanny for a short time (e.g., one week)?

Remember to clarify any gaps in her cv.

Ask for written references. Check that there are some for all her nanny/child-care jobs – if not, ask why not and follow up.

Ask to see original qualification certificates, first-aid certificates, driving licence and passport as proof of her identity.

If she needs to use her own car for the job, check that it has rear seatbelts.

Check that you have the names and telephone numbers of any referees you wish to contact.

Useful ways to finish

If the position is live-in and the interview has gone well, you might choose to show her the room(s) you will be providing for her. This is a good time to talk on a more informal and relaxed basis and to find out more about her.

Give her a good opportunity to ask you any questions she still has. Don't be put off by a nanny who asks lots of questions – it shows that she is thinking carefully about the job.

Explain what will happen next and when you will let her know your decision.

Offer to pay any expenses she has incurred in coming to the interview.

Equal opportunities

It is unlawful to ask questions or to make recruitment decisions that discriminate against anyone because of their sex, marital status, colour, nationality, ethnic origin, disability, religion or sexual orientation.

QUESTIONS YOU CAN AND CAN'T ASK A NANNY AT INTERVIEW

Acceptable questions	Unacceptable questions
How will you manage lifting our two-year-old?	Isn't lifting going to be hard with a damaged back?
If things go well, how long might you want to stay in this job?	Have you any plans to get married? Are you planning to have any children?
We will occasionally require you to start at seven in the morning. How do you feel about that? Will it be possible for you?	What will your husband think if you have to leave early?
	What will you do with your own children?

However, it may be important to know whether someone is physically able to look after your young child, whether she is likely to stay for a reasonable time, or, for a live-out nanny, whether she will be able to start early or spend nights away from her home. To elicit answers to questions like these, you should focus on the requirements of the job, rather than on the personal circumstances of the individual.

Interviewing au pairs over the telephone

While we strongly recommend that you meet your au pair before you make your decision, we recognise that this isn't always possible. So we've provided a list of guidelines and questions for use when interviewing her over the telephone.

Do try, if possible, to get someone who can speak the au pair's native language to do some of the interview for you. This can provide information and nuances you might otherwise miss.

Don't be afraid to spend time considering what she has said and then call her back to clarify any concerns arising from the conversation.

GUIDELINES AND QUESTIONS FOR INTERVIEWING AU PAIRS OVER THE TELEPHONE

Starting the discussion

Introduce yourself and ask her a little about herself. Try to encourage her to relax. Let her know what you want to cover and how long the discussion will take.

Encourage some general chat. This will relax both of you and will help you to get to know her better.

Tell her about yourself, your partner, the children, where you live and how you would expect her to help you around the house and with the children.

Ask her questions arising from what you have read of her personal details.

Useful general questions

Why do you want to be an au pair? What do you hope to gain out of the experience?

What sort of person are you? What makes you easy/difficult to live with?

What do you want from your host family?

What experience do you have of being with children? Of what ages?

What do you enjoy about being with children? What do you like least about being with them?

What type of activities would you like to do with the children?

How often have you been sick in the last year? Do you have any medical conditions that we need to know about?

Do you have any special dietary requirements?

Do you smoke?

What activities would you be happy to help with if you were to come and live with us?

What do you like to cook?

If relevant, ask how she feels about pets.

Useful questions for people who are already au pairs

What do you enjoy least about being an au pair? Why?

What are the best bits? Why?

What is the most difficult situation you have had to handle? What did you do?

Tell me about the type of things you help your host family with at the moment. How do you feel about what you do?

What activities do you enjoy doing with the children you are with at the moment?

What type of food do you cook for them?

Ways to finish

Tell her about the hours and the pocket money and any other benefits, such as holidays. Explain any significant house rules which might affect her decision to come to you (views on overnight guests, use of the telephone, etc.).

Ask her for the names of referees you can speak to.

Ask her about language classes and what she would like to do.

Give her the opportunity to ask you any questions she may have.

Making notes during your interviews

Whether you are interviewing nannies or au pairs, it is useful to think in advance about how you will make notes while you talk. It can be helpful, if you are interviewing several people, to draw up a sheet with the questions you are going to ask and spaces against each section for your comments. You may like to give her a score for each area, which you can record after the interview (perhaps 3 for 'more than competent', 2 for 'competent' and 1 for 'less than competent'). That way you can more easily (and objectively) compare the strengths and weaknesses of a number of people.

CONDUCTING THE INTERVIEWS

There are some key points to bear in mind while carrying out your interviews.

- Begin gently and try to establish a rapport with the nanny. It is not going to help if either of you is too nervous. You want her to relax so that you can see her as she really is. Chat about her journey and perhaps introduce her to the children.
- Explain that you will be making notes during the interview, and tell her how long you expect it to last.
- Make sure that you spend some time early on telling her more about the job. Don't get carried away, though, and spend the whole time talking. On average you should aim to do about 20 per cent of the talking.

- When you ask questions, do so in an inquisitive manner, not in a challenging one. If you are unsure of a response, ask another question to find out more.
- Objectivity is important. To ensure you are objective, you need to ask all candidates the same or broadly similar questions.
- Repeat what the interviewee has said, to check you have understood, and don't be afraid of asking a question and then waiting in silence for a response.
- Be honest about what the job is going to be like. Talk about the possible drawbacks or downsides of the role and discuss any events which might affect it, such as a new baby, house moves, etc. If you are not sure what to mention, you could ask your current nanny for her views.
- Allow the nanny time to ask you questions. Remember this is a two-way process – she is choosing you too. One employer suggested asking previous nannies to write you a reference as an employer, which you can show to nannies during the interviews.
- Trust your instinct or gut feelings, and if you are worried, ask her lots of questions to elicit the information you need to make your decision.
- When you close the interview, explain what will happen next and when you will be able to get back to her.
- Try to take time to chat more informally to the nanny or au pair at the end of the interview, when she is likely to be more relaxed. Having once had a very successful interview with a prospective nanny, we discovered while chatting informally at the end, that she was prone to frequent and severe fainting fits.
- Try not to form a conclusion until after the interview has finished. At this point you might like to check your notes, record your scores (if relevant) and evaluate how you feel overall, before you interview the next person.
- Don't be frightened to appear businesslike. A structured and well-thought-out interview will impress a good nanny.

Employer perspective: Trust your instinct

'We had finished our interviews and there were two people we liked. One nanny seemed to be very outgoing and was hugely outspoken. She seemed a bit more of a risk than the other nanny, but on balance we decided that we liked her the best. It was hard to put a finger on – but we both felt that she would fit into our family. So, we offered her the job and she took it. Eighteen months later, we are glad that we made the decision we did.'

Employer perspective: Honesty is the best policy

'We had interviewed a number of nannies and our favourite was Charlotte. However, in her previous job she had worked for an opera singer and had travelled around the world staying in luxury hotels, with only one little girl to care for. I was concerned that three children, a slightly down-market car and the builders in all year, might not equate with the lifestyle to which she had become accustomed.

'She seemed keen but I asked the agency to check with her that the downsides of the job were acceptable. They did this, and in the end she withdrew. I was disappointed, but it saved us all a lot of heartache in the end.'

Host-family perspective: Niggling doubts

'We had reached the end of our search for an au pair and one person stood out above the rest. She seemed mature and competent and the children liked her. However, I had some niggling doubts.

'When I tried to analyse why, it boiled down to some small points. When I met her she had seemed quite glamorous. She had several long necklaces on and high heels and I found it hard to imagine her playing football or rolling around the floor with the children. She was very concerned about whether her room would be big enough and she criticised her previous host family several times during our discussion.

'In the end, I decided to trust my gut feel and not to ask her to join us. I'll never know if that was the right decision, but on balance it was the one I felt most comfortable with.'

How many interviews do I need to do?

It is a good idea to arrange to see the best two candidates for a subsequent, less formal interview (this is not usually possible for au pairs). In our survey, about half of all employers conducted two or more interviews. The second meeting may last for three or four hours, or even a whole-day or overnight stay. Some employers pay the nanny for her time when she comes to a second interview.

During this extended interview you can let the nanny play with the children and get to know them a bit better; you might ask her to organise an activity (outing/art or craft work) for them. For your part, you can follow up with additional questions on areas you were uncertain about the first time round.

Arrange for the nanny to spend time with your current nanny if relevant (without you there). As well as giving her a chance to find out more about you, you may welcome the views of your current nanny, who will have a good idea of what you are looking for.

You could give the nanny some case study situations, which are relevant to your family, and ask her how she would deal with them. This will test her ability to think through a problem and identify a solution. Remember, though, that it doesn't necessarily tell you how she will respond in a real situation.

EXAMPLE CASE STUDIES

Medical emergency

You are babysitting. The three-year-old has fallen out of his bed and his mouth is bleeding badly. You think his teeth have gone through his bottom lip. The other two children are asleep (one is six and one is three months old). What do you do?

Tantrums

You take the two-year-old to nursery school, where you are expected to leave her for a morning session. When you arrive she has a tantrum and refuses to get out of the car. She cries, kicks and screams, and says she doesn't want to be left. (The baby starts to cry too, because of all the noise.) You get to the nursery door – with difficulty. She is holding on to you tightly, still crying and screaming. It is the first time she has behaved in this way. What do you do?

Sickness?

The parents have gone to work early and the five-year-old wakes up and says he has tummy ache and doesn't want to go to school today. You are not sure if he is telling the truth. The parents didn't mention that he had been poorly in the night. What do you do?

Hospital or school?

You are due to collect the eldest child from school in ten minutes. The second child falls over heavily onto his arm. It looks as if it might be broken and he is screaming. What do you do?

Summer holidays

It's a beautiful day and the first day of the summer holidays. There is a mountain of ironing to do. What do you do?

At the end of the interview, explain what will happen next and make sure you respond by telephone or letter to everyone you see. Whatever you do, respond quickly. After coming this far, it would be awful to lose your first choice because she'd been offered a job elsewhere. If you are still uncertain about who to choose, follow up references for both applicants and see if this helps. Older children will inevitably have their own views and should, perhaps, be involved in your decision. Remember, at the end of the day, to trust your gut feelings or instinct.

A word about what *isn't* said

Part of listening effectively is being aware of what is left unsaid. A nanny who says she loves nannying because it gets her out and about and meeting lots of people, is not saying that she loves it because she loves being with children. This may also be true of course – and a good interviewer will endeavour to find out through subsequent questions.

Observing reactions on faces and body posture/positions is also helpful. Someone who is reluctant to maintain eye contact, and who fidgets and folds her arms or legs or turns away from you, may well be nervous. She may also have something to hide or feel uncomfortable about a particular set of questions. If your questions are fair and reasonable, this may cause you concern.

However, remember not to jump to conclusions. Instead try to tackle the same issue from a different angle until you have satisfied yourself with the outcome. If you are unsure about something, you can always check it out when taking up references.

Typical interview problems/traps

The three main problems for interviewers often arise from forming judgements (positive and negative) about the interviewee too early on in the interview – and therefore not listening properly. Being aware of the traps will help you avoid them.

The first problem is stereotyping. For example, we take a look at the interviewee as she walks up the garden path and decide there and then that she will be too boring for the children/is likely to seduce our partner/is absolutely perfect and probably one of the best nannies there is. We all do this, and there is something to be said for following our intuition. However, try to keep an open mind until the end of the interview.

The second problem is the 'halo' effect, usually felt when we are demoralised by a lack of good applicants, and therefore delighted when an interviewee responds well. Spurred on by our need to find *someone*, we start to assume that everything about her is good and hear what we want to hear, without fully questioning and then testing her responses.

The third problem is where we become amateur psychologists and make judgements about a person's skills based on our own theories of personality. We assume, for example, that someone is bound to love our children and hold strong family values because she still lives at home with her mum. Or we assume that, because she goes to church, she is honest.

Employer perspective: Spoilt for choice?

'We had interviewed a number of potential nannies and had got it down to the final two. They both seemed good and it was hard to choose between them. So we invited each of them back to spend a day with us on two consecutive days. Our current nanny agreed to come along too to help us with our decision. I felt a bit embarrassed to ask the applicants to do this, but I did offer to pay them for their time which made me feel a little better.

'We spent the time doing various activities with the children (painting, playing in the sandpit, doing jigsaws, etc.). I left my current nanny and each applicant together for an hour or so to give them the opportunity to talk about the job, the children and us – warts and all.

'At the end of the two days the better candidate was obvious. She had formed a relationship with the children, was bright and interested and had asked us lots of thoughtful questions.

'It was useful to include our old nanny in the process as she spotted issues which I was then able to check out with the referees. I don't quite know what I'd have done if we had disagreed on the decision – but we didn't, thank goodness!'

Nanny perspective: Who to choose?

'After spending a month looking for a live-in nanny job, I ended up with two job offers. Which I should take seemed clear at first. One family was offering more money and they lived in a lovely house in a nice part of the country. My accommodation was smart and I would have my own bathroom. However, I didn't get a very nice feeling about the family, who seemed cold and formal. Although my rooms were smart they were also impersonal and I wasn't sure I would feel comfortable.

'In the end, I decided to work for the other family, who seemed more friendly. At the interview I had spent some time with the children, who seemed relaxed and confident. Although my room was smaller and I was going to have to share a bathroom with the children, they had just decorated everywhere and had gone to some effort to make it all feel homely. They said I could bring my own pictures and anything else I wanted to make it feel "mine".

'Although some of my friends thought I was nuts, I knew I'd made the right decision. Four years later, I'm still there.'

SUMMARY

- It is important to prepare well for your interviews. You need to check cvs or personal details for any gaps and obvious areas for questioning. Prepare the questions you want to ask at the interview. Decide when to do the interviews and who will be there with you. Develop a view on how much you can pay and the benefits you would like to provide.
- During each interview try to establish a rapport and help the nanny or au pair to relax – you want to see her as she really is. Try to be as objective as possible (having someone else there will help).

- Remember that she is deciding whether to choose you, too. Allow her time to ask you questions.
- It is a good idea to have your best one or two candidates back for a second visit where they spend more time with you and the children on a more informal basis (this is not usually possible for au pairs). It gives you time to follow up on any issues you are uncertain about, gives you the chance to observe them in a more informal setting and see how they relate to the children, and gives them the opportunity to get to know you a bit better.
- If you can't meet an au pair, do make sure that you conduct a thorough telephone interview with her.

4 The Final Stages of Recruitment

'If you have any doubts – don't!' – Mum

'Trust your instinct – but still follow up references thoroughly' – Mum

'Try to speak to previous nannies if you can, to find out what the job's really like' – Nanny

It is easy to get carried away once you have found someone you like and not to check her references in sufficient detail, particularly if her written references are good. However, this last stage is vital. In our survey we asked employers and host families what advice they would give someone about to recruit a nanny or an au pair for the first time. The most frequently mentioned point was to make sure that you follow up references thoroughly.

Once you have checked out the references and have made your decision, you need to formally offer the position to your nanny or au pair. If she accepts the offer, there are a number of other activities that you need to complete before she arrives.

TAKING UP REFERENCES

Because there is no register of nannies or au pairs, it is crucial that you follow up all references rigorously. We recommend that you always speak to two or three referees on the telephone, as people will often give you information that they would be reluctant to put in writing.

Ask the nannies and au pairs to bring copies of their written references to the interview with them (or send them to you). Note what isn't said in the references. For example, if a nanny's sickness record isn't mentioned, this may be because the writer felt that it wasn't important. However, it might be because the nanny was regularly off sick but the referee wanted to be kind or – worse still – to help her to find another job and so leave more quickly. Also note if any jobs are missing references and ask the nanny or the agency why. Agencies can be reluctant to pass on poor references.

Make sure that you follow up written references with a phone call. As a guideline you should call at least two referees who have been involved in the work of the nanny or au pair as recently as possible. If it is the nanny's first job you should be able to call her course tutors and families with whom she did course placements (assuming that she is qualified).

It is easy to follow up and check on course qualifications by ringing the college or course tutor and asking if the nanny did indeed study and pass her qualification there. You can also call the DVLC to check out a driving licence.

It may be more difficult to follow up references of an au pair who hasn't been to the UK before. Some host families ask a friend who speaks the au pair's language to take the references for them. However, it is more difficult to be sure whom you are talking to and to be clear about their relationship to the au pair. One agency said, 'it is notoriously difficult to check out references for au pairs – although we always try our very best. In a sense they come on good faith and you need to make your judgement about them once they start to live with you.'

Remember to ask permission before you telephone a referee, to avoid embarrassing the nanny or au pair with her current employer or host family.

Useful hints and questions when checking references

Ask a general question first, such as 'Tell me about Julie. What was she like as a nanny/au pair?' Listen to what is included and excluded.

Verify the dates in the applicant's cv, and the core facts (the number and ages of children in her care, pay details, etc.).

If there is any aspect of the job or quality that is particularly important to you, ask about it. Remember always to ask open questions, such as 'How caring was Julie?' or 'How was she with the children?' rather than 'She was caring, wasn't she?'

Ask what she was particularly good at, and what her weaker points were. Be insistent when asking about her weaknesses: some people don't like to say. Here are a few questions you can ask.

- If you had to pick one thing that she could have done better, what would it be?
- What would you have liked to change about her? In which areas was she least helpful?
- How did the children feel about her?
- Are there any tips you can give me for managing her?
- How would you describe her attendance? How punctual was she?
- How many days off sick did she have while she worked for you? What type of sickness was it? (This last question is important, as the nanny/au pair may have had many days off for trivial illnesses like colds, or just one absence, for a significant illness which is unlikely to recur, such as an operation.)
- Why did she leave you?
- Would you employ her again? (Watch out for hesitation and a less than convincing 'Yes.' If the referee does sound unsure, you might try: 'You seem unsure. Can I ask why you hesitate?')
- Is there any other information about her that you feel might be relevant to us?

Leave your telephone number with the referee in case they later identify other issues they wish to discuss with you. One employer we came across, who had given their nanny a glowing reference, subsequently discovered she had been dishonest with them, but was unable to contact the new employers.

When you are evaluating the references, remember that what irritates another employer or host family may not annoy you. Listen carefully to the feedback and assess how important it is to you.

As you check several references, be aware of emerging themes. If several host families say that the au pair is quite lazy, it is probably true. However, if only one family says so and the other disagrees, you'll need to read between the lines and ask more questions.

Check what one referee says by asking another for their comments. Don't be afraid of calling twice if you have additional questions.

Checking references can feel awkward and many of us do not enjoy it. But it's worth persevering with the difficult questions, for your own peace of mind.

Employer perspective: Workshy?

'We were about to offer Lucy a job as nanny for our two children and we had three references to check.

'They all gave Lucy excellent references, but they all mentioned that she didn't like to do any housework. This was a tricky one because we didn't expect her to do any general housework, but we did want her to tidy up after the children and complete the normal "nursery duties".

'In the end I shared my concerns with Lucy. I reiterated exactly what we would expect her to do in the house and asked her how she felt about it. I made it very clear that we were delighted with her and would like to employ her, but that the tidying and cleaning up after the children were important aspects of the job. She said she accepted this, and so we took her on.

'In fact, she has turned out to be a great nanny. I don't know if her other employers treated her differently or expected her to do more, or whether she herself has changed, but we haven't had any problems.'

Police Checks (for nannies only)

It is possible for an individual to obtain a police check for themselves (which you can ask to see). There is a minimal charge for this and the forms that need to be completed can be obtained from police stations.

Nanny agencies often insist that nannies obtain a police check, but many remain sceptical about the process. The check only covers the addresses given by the nanny and only looks for convictions from the last five years. It can also take quite a long time to come through. One head of a nanny agency commented that completing a police check could lull employers into a false sense of security and that, though it is helpful, it shouldn't be relied upon.

Conclusion

So, the message is simple. Follow up written references and check them thoroughly. If, after taking up references, you are still unsure about someone, don't take her on.

MAKING AN OFFER

Agreeing the terms and conditions of employment

Call your nanny or au pair as soon as possible after seeing her, to offer her the position over the telephone. If you haven't already been so, now is the time to be specific about the pay or pocket money and the benefits you are offering.

By this stage you will have a good idea of the pay/package your nanny is expecting and the extent to which you can satisfy her requirements. If she is unhappy with the pay you are offering, you may be able to entice her with some of the benefits, such as the accommodation (for a live-in nanny), the hours, holidays abroad, and so on. You may want to promise her a pay rise in six months' time if things work out well – which buys you a bit more time. More about pay and benefits can be found in Chapters 8 and 9.

Probationary periods

It is common to agree a probationary period with your nanny, during which either party can terminate the arrangement with little notice (usually one week). This gives you flexibility should she prove to be unsuitable. If you are using an agency, it is a good idea to align your probationary period with the one the agency sets. That way, you may replace an unsuitable nanny for a minimal charge, providing you do so within the agreed period.

The offer letter

Once your nanny has accepted the job, you should write her a formal offer of employment. Some employers choose to send their written contract of employment to the nanny at this stage; others give it to her during her first week. See Chapter 5 for more information about contracts of employment.

> **SAMPLE JOB OFFER LETTER FOR A LIVE-OUT NANNY**
>
> Dear Julie
>
> We are delighted to be able to offer you the job of nanny for our two children. We would like you to start on Monday, 1 February, and spend a week doing the job alongside our current nanny, Emma, who leaves at the end of that week.
>
> We will pay you £X, net of tax and National Insurance, for a 50-hour week. If we ask you to baby-sit for us or to work any overtime, it will be paid at an hourly (net) rate of £X. We will review your salary on 1 January each year.
>
> We have attached your contract of employment with further details of your hours, holidays, etc., as discussed during your interview.
>
> We are delighted that you are coming to work for us and we look forward to getting to know you better over the coming months. If you have any queries or concerns before 1 February, please do call us.
>
> Yours sincerely,

Au pairs from non-EU countries, who are travelling to the UK for the first time, will need a letter of invitation from you in order to obtain visas/permission to enter the country. Your au pair agency will be able to give you an example of what to write. Some of the basic things to include are:

- Your address
- The au pair's name
- The dates when the position will start and end
- The language you speak at home
- The occupation of the parents, and the number and ages of the children
- Details of your pets, if any
- The rooms available for the au pair's use

- The weekly allowance/pocket money you will pay her
- The total hours you will require her to work, and the free time she will have
- The types of tasks you want her to do
- Some details about language classes and whether you will contribute towards their cost
- A little about your family's hobbies and interests, and the location of your home
- A family photograph

SAMPLE OFFER LETTER FOR AN AU PAIR

Dear Maria

We are delighted to be able to ask you to come to be our au pair from 1 October to 31 March. As you know, we have three children, Jessica (10), Alex (9) and Lauren (7). I am a GP (doctor) and I work locally three days a week. My husband works as a manager in a computer company in the City. We speak English in our home, although both my husband and I can speak a little French. Our children all attend our local school, which is about ten minutes' walk away. We have a dog and a cat who live with us too!

We will provide you with your own bedroom and ask you to share the bathroom with the children. We will give you £X pocket money each week, and will ask you to help us out for five hours a day, Monday to Friday. In addition, we might ask you to baby-sit up to twice a week. Your weekends will normally be free.

We would like you to help with taking the children to and from school and, on the days when I work, with preparing meals for them, looking after them and encouraging them to do their homework until I arrive home. We would also like you to help with the ironing, general tidying up and light cleaning.

Your language classes will be held twice a week at our local college, which is about fifteen minutes' walk away or a short bus journey. We will pay half the cost of the classes, the total cost of which will be £X.

As a family, we enjoy walking and visiting interesting places. We would like you to join us in these activities. We enjoy cycling and have a bicycle you can use if you want to come with us. Our town has many attractions. There is a lovely park and plenty of things to do – swimming baths, tennis courts, cinemas, etc.

I enclose a photograph of the family so you can see what we all look like. We look forward to you hearing from you about your travel plans and to meeting you on 1 October.

Kind regards,

Turning people down

Once your new nanny or au pair has accepted the position, you should contact all the others you have interviewed and inform them of your decision. Doing it this way round allows you to hold onto your second choice until you are sure that your first choice has accepted the offer.

When you speak or write to the people you have rejected, it is important to be honest and helpful if you can, without undermining their confidence any more than is necessary.

EXAMPLE REJECTION LETTER

Dear Catherine,

Thank you for taking the time to come to see us yesterday. We enjoyed meeting you and were impressed with the way you responded to the children.

However, on balance, we have decided to offer the position to a nanny who has had more experience of working with three children.

Thank you again – and we wish you well in your future career.

Yours sincerely,

PREPARING FOR THE ARRIVAL OF YOUR NEW NANNY OR AU PAIR

Spending a little time getting ready for your nanny or au pair's arrival is invaluable, as it will indicate to her that she is important to you. The first few days of her time with you will set the tone for your relationship. You may wish to:

- Make sure your accommodation is ready (if appropriate). For a live-in nanny or au pair, you may want to have a phone line put in for her personal use.
- Find out about local language schools/classes (for an au pair) and enrol her, if appropriate.

- Ensure you are adequately insured in the home to cover your nanny/au pair's safety. You should have employer and public-liability insurance. (Many household insurance policies automatically provide this, but it is worth checking.) You may need to arrange additional cover for your nanny or au pair's belongings. Check on cover for other people in your home too – for example, when your nanny invites other nannies to visit her. If your nanny will be bringing her own child to work with her, check that they are both covered under your policy. And if you are supplying a car, make sure it is serviced and insured for her to use at work with the children.
- Check whether your nanny has public liability insurance or professional negligence cover (this is not appropriate for au pairs). The Professional Association of Nursery Nurses (PANN) will be able to provide her with details about it (see Useful Contacts).
- Make a list of important telephone numbers (your/your partner's work and mobile numbers, doctors and dentist, hospital, schools, nurseries, etc.).
- Prepare a checklist of the daily routine, which your nanny or au pair might find useful until she establishes herself.
- Ask your current nanny or au pair to write down any recipes that the children like. Also ask her to write down any rules that she has for the children (for example, they must wash their hands before they eat).
- Plan the first week and, if you can, arrange an overlap with the current nanny (not so appropriate for au pairs).
- Have a spare set of keys cut.
- Provide a credit card for her job-related expenses.

Employer perspective: Caution pays

'Our nanny invited a friend of hers to lunch at our house. The friend brought the child that she looked after. Unfortunately, the child pulled a very hot pot of tea over himself while the nannies were in the kitchen. The child was badly injured. Our own children were in bed asleep when the accident occurred. We were told that we were going to be sued by the child's parents, who were blaming our nanny. The whole situation was dreadful. At one point our solicitors wrote to us to say that our household insurance policy did not cover accidents caused by employees in the home, and we would be personally liable for the costs and damages which could amount to thousands of pounds if the case was successful. Thankfully, we discovered that the policy had been updated specifically to cover employees in the home. However, it is worth noting that it only covered our employee for accidents that happened in our own home and not in anyone else's. We've since done some research and taken out a more comprehensive insurance policy for our nanny.'

Nanny-share arrangements

If you are entering into a nanny-share arrangement, there are a number of things you need to think about beforehand and discuss and agree with the other family:

- Whether the nanny will work at your house or the other family's or both on an alternating basis.
- The role, house rules and routine.
- How you'll share the cost.
- How you'll handle administrative details such as pay, tax and National Insurance.
- Insurance cover – the other family's children may not be covered in your car, home, etc.
- Notice and cover for holidays.
- What happens if your children or the nanny should be ill?
- What happens if one set of parents are late home and the child is at the other family's house?
- How you provide feedback to the nanny about what is going well and less well.

If you don't know the other family very well, spend some time getting to know each other by socialising together. In our experience, nanny-share arrangements between friends are more successful than those between acquaintances.

SUMMARY

- Checking references thoroughly is vital. You need to check at least two recent ones by talking to the referee over the telephone – written references are not sufficient. This applies to both nannies and au pairs.
- You need to agree the basic terms with your nanny and au pair (pay, pocket money, hours, etc.) and then send her a letter to confirm your conversation.
- Before she arrives, there are a number of things you can do to prepare. Being well prepared will give her the impression that she is important to you. This will help you to begin the relationship on the right footing.

Part II:

Managing the Relationship

5 Setting the Relationship up for Success

'Find out as much as you can early on about the children's routine, the parents' approach to discipline, places you can visit, etc.' – Nanny

'It's worth spending time in the first week setting everything up with your nanny.' – Mum

'Be sure of the ground rules. It is difficult to backpedal – and far easier to relax things once trust has been established.' – Mum

The first few days are critical because they set the tone for your relationship with your new nanny or au pair. It is important to plan her first week with you, as there will be a lot of information that you need to impart. The children may be feeling wobbly, because things are changing for them too, and it is vital to think about what will help them get used to the new nanny or au pair. At the end of the first week, it is essential to sit down and review how things have gone, in an open and honest way.

THE EMOTIONAL SIDE

When a new nanny or au pair starts, it can be an unsettling time. The parents, children and nanny or au pair all find themselves treading carefully around each other for the first few weeks. You may also be dealing with other emotions. For example, if you've replaced a nanny or au pair you really liked, you are having to deal with that loss at the same time as adjusting to the new person. Or if you had a bad experience with your previous nanny or au pair, you may be feeling vulnerable and rather negative towards nannies and au pairs in general. You need to be careful not to punish the new person for the previous one's misdemeanours.

It is important to invest time getting to know your new nanny or au pair in the first few days. Ask her how she is feeling, so that she can tell you if she is homesick. An au pair, particularly if she is in the UK for the first time, needs looking after. Take her out and show her the local sights. Include her in family life. Be prepared to listen to her life story and problems, and find her some friends, preferably other au pairs living close by, to prevent her from becoming lonely.

Employer perspective: The halo effect

'My departing nanny, Suzanne, was an excellent nanny but left to pursue a different career. I found it difficult to adapt to my new nanny. I kept comparing the two of them and seeing my new nanny in a less favourable way. I thought I'd made a mistake and should have interviewed more people. I talked to the children to identify what was missing and realised that there was nothing from the children's point of view, only from mine. My old nanny had become a friend and I missed her company. My new nanny was unlikely to fulfil that role because we had less in common. Once I recognised that I was experiencing Suzanne's departure as a loss, I was able to accept our new nanny and identify some unique qualities that she brought to the job, such as her great flexibility and willingness. These were things which I had previously overlooked.'

Host-family perspective: The horns effect

'I had to ask my au pair to leave before Christmas because she was very lazy and didn't enjoy being with the children. She was very grumpy and unhappy and I disliked the atmosphere it caused in the house. When my new au pair, Jitka, started, I found it difficult to trust her. I kept thinking about my previous au pair and anticipating that she would behave in the same way. As a consequence, I was more distant and less trusting with Jitka than I would normally be. Jitka asked me if I was happy with her. That made me realise that I'd been punishing her for my old au pair's behaviour, which was unfair. I decided to write down my experiences with my old au pair in order to exorcise them from my mind. I then made a big effort to show Jitka around and form a good relationship with her. She turned out to be fantastic. She was full of energy and really good with the children. She was not at all like my old au pair, and I felt enthusiastic about having au pairs again.'

THE HANDOVER PERIOD (NANNIES ONLY)

If you are employing a nanny for the first time, we advise you to spend a lot of time with her during the first few days, to familiarise her with the job. Gradually leave your children with her, so that they get to know one another and she can develop her own routine.

If you have already have a nanny, arrange a handover between the departing nanny and the new one. Typically, handover periods last from a couple of days to one week. In our survey, only 43 per cent of employers organised an overlap with the previous nanny, and over 30 per cent of nannies considered that the overlap had been too short.

A handover period has several advantages.

- Your departing nanny has the opportunity to explain the children's routine and pass on tips to the new nanny.
- The children can see the two nannies working together, and they have time to get used to the new nanny while they still have the security of the departing nanny being around.
- You and your departing nanny will get the chance to see the

new nanny in action and discuss any minor development needs or more serious concerns about her suitability for the job.

- Your current nanny can introduce the new one to some of her friends. This is particularly important if the new nanny hasn't worked in your area before.
- It saves you time. Your departing nanny can take the new nanny round the house, show her how to use essential equipment, and do a tour of the neighbourhood for you.

There can be disadvantages to a handover period, too. You have to pay both nannies for their services; and, if you are not satisfied with your departing nanny's performance, you may worry that she will teach the new nanny bad habits or that she might be rude about you.

Don't be put off having a handover period if your last nanny wasn't a complete success. In our experience, the departing nanny will usually put on a good show for the new one, because she wants to appear competent. Make sure you spend time with your new nanny, explaining the role – what is and isn't acceptable, and the house rules. In the process, you should avoid criticising the departing nanny, however tempting it is, as this will reflect badly on you.

Employer perspective: A breath of fresh air

'We changed our nanny, Sarah, after five years. Sarah had a large network of nanny friends in the area. She had been an excellent nanny but some of her nanny friends were tiresome. They seemed to spend a lot of time gossiping about their employers and comparing terms and conditions. The nannies didn't keep their views to themselves either, and would often pass on information that I'd rather not know. On her last evening with us, Sarah took Vicky, our new nanny, out for a drink to introduce her to the nanny crowd. My heart sank. I wanted a new nanny and a new circle of friends for the children. I said nothing and needn't have worried. Vicky's eyes were opened straight away when one nanny remarked, "You'll never cope with the job, you know." She decided that she didn't feel comfortable with them and she formed her own network through the children's school. She established relationships with mums as well as nannies and au pairs, and I liked her friends without exception.'

DISCUSSING THE ROLE

Although you may have described the job to your nanny or au pair during the interview, it is vital to discuss it again during the first few days. Our survey showed that, in general, nannies and au pairs felt less informed about the job than employers and host families thought they were.

INFORMATION PROVIDED BY EMPLOYERS AND HOST FAMILIES TO NANNIES AND AU PAIRS

Information provided to nanny/au pair by employer/host family	% of employers of nannies providing information	% of nannies receiving information	% of host families providing information	% of au pairs receiving information
Role and responsibilities	98	89	100	71
House rules	82	63	90	76
Local amenities	91	76	93	71
How to use household equipment	91	83	97	81
Emergency contact numbers	100	89	93	76

What the role entails

Discuss what the job involves. For example:

- Hours: what's the latest time the nanny will finish. It is better to make the hours sound worse than they will be in practice. Your nanny or au pair will be pleased if she can occasionally finish earlier than expected.
- Daily responsibilities such as school runs, visits to the doctor, dentist and clinic, washing, ironing and mending children's clothes, changing the children's beds, shoe cleaning, preparing and cooking nutritious, balanced meals, keeping bedrooms and play areas clean and tidy, cleaning and tidying the bathroom and kitchen after use by the children, sterilising bottles, cleaning baby equipment and doing light children's shopping.
- Organising activities: planning and carrying out educational and fun activities, for example, arts and crafts, outings to appropriate places, reading, cooking, dressing up, music and having friends to play. Also allowing the children to have quieter times by themselves and appropriate sleep periods.
- Keeping a diary of appointments. Some parents like the nanny or au pair to record activities undertaken so that they are kept informed about how the children have spent the day.
- Preparing a weekly shopping list for the children's and nanny's or au pair's food and other requirements.
- Providing feedback to the parents at the end of each day about how the children have been, what they have done and any other relevant issues, for example, school matters.
- Ensuring that homework is done properly and that the children are not too exhausted to do it.
- Liaising with the school on behalf of the parents.
- Dressing the children in the morning and bathing them at the end of the day.
- Accompanying the family on outings and holidays from time to time (live-in nannies and au pairs).
- Baby-sitting as agreed at interview.
- Household tasks agreed at interview.

What you don't want to happen

There may be things that you want to ask your nanny or au pair not to do. For example:

- If you don't want her to finish work as soon as you get home, agree a daily handover period, which allows you to change clothes if necessary, do essential jobs and communicate about the children's day.
- Too much activity and socialising might restrict the children from playing by themselves and using their imagination. You may wish to provide guidance on the number of friends invited to play each week. Some nannies or au pairs go the other way and don't do enough socialising.
- You may not want friends of your nanny or au pair coming round to visit during the day, without children of similar ages. These relationships should be fostered during the nanny's or au pair's private time.
- If nannies or au pairs talk among themselves a lot, there's a risk of their ignoring the children. Ask your nanny or au pair to play with the children and ensure that all activities are child-focused.
- Think about how often you would like your children to get some fresh air and provide a guideline, so you can be sure they don't stay indoors all the time.
- There may be activities that you disapprove of or would like to ration, such as trips to McDonald's, doing personal shopping during working hours, the children watching television and videos, playing with the computer, etc.
- If your nanny or au pair has strong views, for example, on religion or politics, you might want her to keep them to herself while at work.
- The day must be organised around the children's needs. For example, if your children need a sleep in the afternoon, and your nanny or au pair gets some respite, that's fine. But if they don't, she shouldn't make them go to bed so that she can have a rest.
- If a child doesn't like a particular type of food, she shouldn't force him to eat it, and risk mealtimes becoming a battlefield.

It is good practice to prepare a job description for the nanny and to go through it during your discussion. An example of a job description for a live-out nanny is given in Chapter 2, and a more detailed job description for a live-in nanny is given in Appendix II. Job descriptions are not really appropriate for au pairs, however, many families recommend drawing up and agreeing a list of activities that your au pair will be responsible for.

ESTABLISHING THE HOUSE RULES

It can be embarrassing discussing the house rules at the start of your relationship. If you do feel self conscious about it, acknowledge this to your nanny or au pair and stress how important it is to have a common understanding of what is and isn't acceptable from day one. Any house rules, that could result in disciplinary action being taken if they are broken, should also be stated in the contract of employment. The house rules will differ depending on whether your nanny lives with you or not. Therefore, we have provided ideas for house rules under three headings, general house rules, house rules for live-in carers and house rules for the employer and host family.

GENERAL HOUSE RULES FOR ALL CARERS

Drink, drugs and smoking
Typically, do not drink alcohol, smoke or take any other drugs while you are with the children, or be with people who are doing so.

Disciplining the children
Agree how the nanny/au pair should deal with difficult behaviour, e.g. by time-outs, distracting the child, withdrawing treats. This will vary according to your own views and the ages of the children. Most parents make it clear that the nanny/au pair should not smack the children in any circumstances.

Use of the house
Are certain rooms (e.g., your living room) out of bounds or available only at certain times?

Use of the phone at work

Are private phone calls allowed? If so, in what circumstances and what quantity?

Sickness

When and how would you like the nanny/au pair to inform you when she is sick? Explain how difficult it will be for you to organise cover or take time off work yourself.

Holidays

How much notice do you require for holidays?

Accidents and breakages

She should deal with the children first and ensure their safety, then report all accidents and breakages as soon as possible.

Communal household tasks

What would you like her to share responsibility for in the house (e.g., filling and emptying the dishwasher)?

Visits from friends

Some parents like to be told in advance, others are happy to leave this up to the nanny/au pair. In either case, it does no harm to point out that all visits should be built around the children's needs.

Food and drink

Do you expect her to eat with the children? Is any food or drink for the parents' use only?

Confidentiality

It is important to be clear about what is covered by the term 'confidentiality'. A working definition might be: 'Conversations with us, and information in any way connected with us, are to be treated as confidential. Any breach of confidentiality will lead to disciplinary action.'

Expenses

How much are you willing to provide for activities and treats? Where do you wish the kitty to be kept and do you want any receipts/ records kept of how the money is spent?

Use of the car at work
When is it available? Does she need to use child seats? Who is responsible for keeping it clean and filling it with petrol and oil? What should she do if she is involved in an accident?

Standard of dress
If you have any views on this, now is the time to share them.

HOUSE RULES FOR LIVE-IN CARERS

Visitors and overnight guests
Can your nanny/au pair have visitors outside work hours? Do you want her to introduce her visitors to you? Can friends and boyfriends stay overnight? Some employers/host families forbid any overnight guests; others allow female friends to stay. Boyfriends are a controversial issue. Some families ban male overnight guests; others take a more liberal approach and allow steady boyfriends to stay the night. Whatever your views, be honest about them.

Evenings
Are you happy for a nanny/au pair to be around in the evenings? Can she join you for your evening meal? When do you need private time? If you do not want her around, think what you need to provide to facilitate this. Some employers/host families put a fridge, kettle, phone and television in the nanny/au pair's bedroom so that she is more self-contained.

Use of phone for personal calls
Can she make private calls in the evenings, and, if so, who pays for them? Options include: paying for a specified number of calls (e.g., a couple of calls home a week for up to 15 minutes); giving her an allowance (e.g., £20 worth of calls per quarter); you paying for all local calls and charging her for the long-distance ones or providing her with a private phone line which she pays for.

Cars
If you provide her with a car, can she use it in her private time? Who pays for petrol for private use? If she gets a parking fine or

has an accident, what should she do and who is responsible for the cost? Remind her of the law on drinking and driving, particularly if she is not from the UK.

Provision of food and drink
Are you buying all her food? Is there a limit to what she can ask for?

Use of shared facilities
Will she need to share her bathroom and any other facilities with others? Who is responsible for cleaning her bedroom and the facilities she uses? If she shares the bathroom with you, would you like her to avoid using it at certain times of the day?

Drinking and smoking
Can she drink and smoke after work in your house? If so, where?

Registering with a local doctor and dentist
Ask her to register quickly so that she can receive immediate treatment if necessary.

Midweek socialising
Do you mind what time she comes in when she has been out in the evenings? For example, some employers/host families ask their nanny/au pair to be in by midnight during the week.

HOUSE RULES FOR THE EMPLOYER AND HOST FAMILY

You will pay on time at the agreed rates.

You will give as much notice as you can of any changes in hours of work or lateness.

You will not undermine the nanny's/au pair's authority with the children, if you have different views.

You will treat the nanny/au pair with respect, and treat all personal matters relating to her as confidential.

You will provide and seek regular feedback about how the job is going.

You will always leave contact numbers in case of an emergency.

SHARING IMPORTANT INFORMATION ABOUT THE CHILDREN

It is essential to share with your nanny or au pair important information about the children's routines, medical conditions, personalities and development needs.

Routines

You need to describe the children's routine to your new nanny or au pair. This is something you could delegate to your existing nanny if you have arranged a handover period. The areas that should be covered are:

- The daily routine, with an hour-by-hour description of each child's day, including what time they wake up or need to be woken, mealtimes, bathtime and bedtime.
- The school routine: drop-off and pick-up times each day, and what equipment each child requires.
- The school holiday routine or activities.
- Extra-curricular activities for each child, e.g., piano lessons.
- Nursery duties and any household tasks that you agreed at interview.

It is useful to write this down as a list or timetable so that the nanny or au pair can refer to it during the first few weeks. A description of a daily routine and a schedule of weekly activities are given in Appendix III.

Medical conditions

Explain any medical conditions your children have, how the conditions manifest themselves and what medication they require. Tell the nanny or au pair what to watch out for and what steps she should take if the condition occurs or worsens. Show her the medication, demonstrate how it should be taken, observe her doing it and provide feedback. Provide a list of emergency numbers and inform her about any clinics that you or she might need to attend.

Personalities

Describe your children's personalities to the new nanny or au pair. Tell her about their temperaments and typical behaviour, about triggers for temper tantrums and appropriate ways of dealing with and avoiding them. Explain what foods they like and dislike, and the games and activities that each child enjoys. Give her tips on how to respond if the children are upset or tired, including the use of comforters, and let her know about people who are important to them, such as friends or grandparents.

Development needs

Discuss what stage the children are at in their development, what is important for them at the moment and how you see them changing over the next six to twelve months. For example:

Simon, aged 7

- He will be taking his exams in two months' time so he needs to focus on his homework. Restrict his friends' visits to twice a week during termtime.
- He is becoming more independent. Give him some freedom, e.g., using his pocket money to buy things at the shops.
- He can take responsibility for simple tasks and errands. Ask him to help, e.g., by feeding the goldfish or setting the table, and praise him for doing so.
- He is going through a growth spurt. Provide a snack when he returns home from school.
- During school holidays arrange sporting activities for him so that he can let off steam.

Elizabeth, aged 2

- She is starting nursery in six months' time and so she needs to be potty trained.
- Phase out her morning sleeps.
- Train her to use a glass.
- She has been slow with her speech development and needs practice, e.g. sing songs together; read her stories and ask her to tell you what happened afterwards.

- Increase her social activities so that she gets used to mixing with other children of her age, and sharing her toys.

DESCRIBING YOUR HOUSE, EQUIPMENT AND LOCAL AREA

To help your new nanny or au pair to settle in quickly, you need to familiarise her with your house and equipment and the area where you live. If you already have a nanny and have organised a handover period, you could delegate this responsibility to your departing nanny.

The house and equipment

Give her a tour of the house and explain which rooms are for the children's use and any that are out of bounds. Point out key pieces of equipment she'll need to use, for example the dishwasher, washing machine, tumble drier, iron and ironing board; kitchen equipment such as kettle, toaster, oven and fridge/freezer; baby equipment; the car and children's car seats; the computer and other children's games; the telephone system and burglar alarm.

The local area

It is important to introduce your nanny or au pair to key people like nursery staff, teachers and friends. You should also take her round the area and point out important places such as the doctor, dentist, baby clinic and nearest hospital for accident and emergencies; local amenities such as parks, shops, play groups, sports centres, and venues for extra-curricular classes; nurseries and schools and the houses where your children's special friends live. You can also take the opportunity to check that your nanny or au pair can drive safely, if appropriate.

SORTING OUT THE ADMINISTRATIVE DETAILS (NANNIES ONLY)

Once your nanny has started the job, there is some paperwork that needs to be done. The key things are to provide a written contract of employment, if you haven't already done so, and to discuss and agree how you will pay her salary, tax, National Insurance, and provide any benefits.

Written contract of employment

By law, you must provide your nanny with a written statement of the main terms and conditions of employment (unless she has been employed on a temporary contract for less than a month), within two months of starting the job. However, it is good practice to give her the contract before she starts with you, or during her first few days. Our survey showed that 75 per cent of nannies have a written contract of employment.

KEY CONTENTS OF A WRITTEN CONTRACT OF EMPLOYMENT

Personal details

The names and addresses of the nanny and the employer, the date of issue of the contract, the date of the end of the contract (for fixed term/temporary staff), the date of commencement of the employment (and previous service, if any, counting towards continuous employment), the job title, and the place of work.

Remuneration

This is usually the net weekly salary, the intervals at which it will be paid, the frequency of salary reviews, and the date of the next review. Plus any benefits that will be provided.

Probationary period

Often one month.

Hours of work

The standard working hours each week, any weekend work and baby-sitting.

Holidays

Bank holidays plus paid holidays. The legal minimum is four weeks. Many employers ask their nanny to take a certain number of weeks at a time specified by them. You need to state that holiday entitlement will be calculated on a pro-rata basis in your nanny's final year.

Sickness and injuries
Statutory Sick Pay (SSP) plus any additional sick pay you are prepared to pay when your nanny is ill (e.g., two weeks at full pay).

Terminating the contract
The notice periods during the probationary period (e.g., one week) and afterwards (e.g., one month). By law, after two years' continuous employment, you must give one week's additional notice for each year of continuous employment, up to a maximum of twelve weeks.

Confidentiality clause

Pension
You need to state if you provide a pension scheme or not. In practice, it is rare for a pension scheme to be provided.

Disciplinary rules
Examples of gross and serious misconduct, the disciplinary warnings procedure, and the appeals process.

Grievance and appeals procedures
Ask her to air any concerns immediately, and state to whom (e.g. a family solicitor, local GP or nanny agency). It is important that your disciplinary process has a right of appeal so that, in the event of you dismissing your nanny, a tribunal would view it as fair.

Signatures

Some contracts also include a job description and a description of the facilities the employer will provide. Nanny agencies often supply employers with sample contracts of employment. We advise you to check that any sample forms you are given include all the information given above. An example of a contract (for a live-in nanny) is given in Appendix IV.

When you are happy with the draft contract, show it to your nanny, discuss the terms and conditions stated in it, make any agreed changes, and then both sign it. You should each keep a copy. Normally, contracts of employment cover one year, and if your nanny stays longer you will need to update it. If you make changes to the contract during the year, the nanny should be given a written statement of the changes as soon as possible, and in any case, no later than a month after they are made.

Pay

At the interview, you will have agreed a rate of pay. Now the nanny has started work, you need to discuss and confirm the following:

- *How you will pay her* – cash, cheque, standing order or a combination of these. If you are going to set up a standing order, you will need her bank or building society details.
- *Payday* – some nannies are happy to be paid monthly, others like to be paid weekly.
- *Salary increases* – how often salary reviews will take place. Annually is the norm, but some employers provide smaller, bi-annual increases or may increase the salary mid-year following a change to the job, for instance if the nanny takes responsibility for a new baby.
- *Tax and National Insurance contributions* – what they will be based upon and how often they'll be paid.
- *Benefits* – what benefits you will provide.

REVIEWING THE FIRST FEW DAYS

The first few days of a new relationship are stressful for both parties, and so it is important for you to sit down and talk about how it is working. As the manager of a nanny agency said, 'Often issues occur very early on in the relationship and, if these are not ironed out straight away, the employer and employee become wary of each other.' Our survey showed that only 34 per cent of nannies and 24 per cent of au pairs found that the job was exactly as described at interview. Furthermore, over 50 per cent of employers of nannies and 70 per cent of host families found that the nanny or au pair did not fully meet their expectations on starting the job.

The most common areas of tension for employers in the early days are:

- How the nanny spends her time with the children, in particular whether the activities she has organised meet the children's needs or her own social needs.
- How untidy the nanny leaves areas of the house, for example, the kitchen.
- General lack of initiative and common sense.
- Poor attention to nursery duties such as keeping children's rooms tidy, washing, ironing and putting clothes away.

The most common concerns for new nannies and au pairs in the early days are:

- Longer working hours than were specified at interview, and additional hours being required at short notice.
- More household tasks – for example, cleaning and family ironing – than were agreed during the interview.
- For au pairs, less help from the mother than expected.
- For nannies, a lower salary and fewer benefits than agreed at interview.
- For nannies, not having sole charge of the children; the parents being around and interfering too much.
- Less freedom than expected: what a nanny or au pair can and can't do with the children often isn't apparent until she starts work.
- For au pairs, feeling lonely and homesick, particularly in the first few weeks.

The most common concerns for host families in the early days are:

- The au pair being homesick.
- Poor attention to housework.
- Lack of interest in the children.
- Difficulty communicating, poor English-language skills.
- The au pair being withdrawn and staying in her room.

We should also point out that some employers and host families in our survey were delighted to find that their nanny or au pair exceeded their expectations from the start.

The discussion

When you review the early days, it is importa conversation away from the children, so that both of to air your views openly. At the start, help your nanny or give you her views by asking her some open-ended question example, 'How have you found your first few days?' 'What aspects have you enjoyed?' 'We all find some things challenging. What aspects have you found difficult?' 'What would help?' 'Is there anything, however small, that you feel might become an issue over time?'

Then you need to give your views about what you think is working well, and what you would like to see instead. Be as specific as possible and give examples. Let her know of any other niggles or concerns.

At the end of the discussion, summarise any actions to be taken on either side, and agree when you'll next formally review how it's going. Ideally, this should be within the next fortnight.

Employer perspective: A bad start

'Our nanny crashed our Volvo estate into the neighbour's wall on her first day in the job. It was very unnerving. I was very upset about it and felt like ending the relationship immediately. On reflection, I decided that driving was only one aspect of the job and, as she'd been working overseas for two years, she was obviously out of practice. We talked about it and we agreed to arrange and pay for a double driving lesson for her and to provide a smaller vehicle for her to drive. After the lesson, I asked the driving instructor for his views and he said that she could drive, but her skills were rather rusty. It's been eighteen months now and she is still with us. She has proved to be a good and caring nanny. It took me longer to trust her than my previous nannies, but I am glad that I gave her a second chance.'

Employer perspective: Changed appearance

'I was pleased with my choice of nanny, Helen – she seemed perfect in many ways. The only thing that I was unsure about was her appearance. At interview she'd worn a smart skirt and top, but when she started work her clothes were quite different. She dressed in "Grunge" style and she started to streak her hair fuchsia pink. If I'm honest about it, at first I found it quite embarrassing because I was concerned about what other mothers might think. At the end of the first week, I talked to Helen about her tastes and lifestyle and understood why she wanted to express her individuality. I realised that she still had the skills and personality that had impressed me at interview; only her appearance had changed. Helen stayed for three years and was a breath of fresh air for the children.'

TIPS FOR ESTABLISHING A GOOD RELATIONSHIP

Our survey generated some excellent tips (given verbatim below) for establishing a good relationship from the start with nannies and au pairs. Why not share them with your new nanny or au pair? It might help to establish an open and honest relationship.

ESTABLISHING A GOOD RELATIONSHIP FROM THE START WITH YOUR NANNY

Tips for employers of nannies from other employers of nannies	Tips for nannies from other nannies
Make more rules rather than less, so that you know where you are from the start. It is easier to relax things once trust has been established.	Get a written contract of employment. Ask about the house rules, disciplining the children, etc.

Tips for employers of nannies from other employers of nannies	Tips for nannies from other nannies
Spend time up front understanding each other's needs and setting up standards and structures.	Don't be talked into anything you don't want to do. Only look after the children. Set the boundaries and let the family know what you need from them. It makes for a happier household.
If you have an experienced nanny, establish what tasks and duties you want performed, rather than leaving it up to her. You can't add new jobs as you go along very easily.	Don't be over-familiar with your employers too soon.
Let your nanny take responsibility straight away.	Don't always insist on sole charge straight away. You can learn a lot working alongside a parent, even if you don't agree with how they do things.
Some younger nannies need emotional support themselves early on, especially if they are a long way from home.	Check that they are paying your tax and National Insurance.
Remember it's a two-way relationship – find out what they want from you.	Get in touch with your nanny agency and find other nannies in the area, to ensure you don't get lonely.
Accept that they will do things differently. Focus on how they look after your children, rather than on how they load the dishwasher.	Watch the parents. Learn how they relate to the children. Don't go into the job like a bull in a china shop. Be the children's friend as well as their nanny.

ESTABLISHING A GOOD RELATIONSHIP FROM THE START WITH YOUR AU PAIR

Tips for host families from other host families

Draw up a detailed list of activities, so that your au pair knows what is expected of her. Ask her to be flexible, too.

Set simple and clear house rules from the outset.

Accept that you have another person in your family and home.

Spend four to six weeks settling in the new au pair, and don't be too judgemental about her abilities early on.

Remember that au pairs are young and need support.

Except in emergencies, their English classes should come first.

Make them welcome and give them private space. Welcome their friends, too.

Provide food they like, even if it's not to your taste.

Be flexible. Some au pairs like to spend time with the family, others are very independent.

Find other young people for them to see. You're middle-aged to them.

Give feedback immediately; nip things in the bud.

Tips for au pairs from other au pairs

Ask the family if they like your work and if they are happy with you.

Don't start work without a clear and fair contract.

Be prepared – it's not a dream job!

At the beginning, agree on rules which should be kept at all times.

The start is very difficult – you have to be friendly and patient. It is important to get to know your family well.

A final, cheeky tip: 'Don't show your family how hard-working you are!'

Tips for host families from other host families

Expect them to do as much as you could, not more. Make them part of your family and don't treat them as slaves.

Accept that they may have little household or child-care experience.

Enable your au pair to spend time away from the family, so that you can all have a break from each other.

SUMMARY

- It is normal to find it unsettling when a new nanny or au pair starts.
- Establish a handover period with your departing nanny if you can. If not, arrange to spend time with your new nanny during the first few days, so that you can hand over responsibility to her gradually.
- Go through the role, both what it involves and what you don't want to happen.
- Explain the house rules and what you'll guarantee in return.
- Describe the children's routines, medical conditions, personalities and development needs.
- Sort out the administrative details, including a written contract of employment.
- Familiarise your nanny or au pair with the house and equipment and with the area.

- Spend lots of time early on, settling your nanny or au pair in, and introduce her to some other local nannies or au pairs.
- Carry out a review of the first week, and be as open and honest as possible with each other.

6 Communicating with Your Nanny or Au Pair

'Respect your nanny and her expertise. She is a professional.' – Dad

'Your relationship with the parents is vital – so that the child has stability and you are happy.' – Nanny

'Talk with your family a lot – about the children and about whether they are happy with you.' – Au pair

'Talk to your nanny, give her time, listen to her and show her that she matters to you.' So said one employer in our survey. It sounds obvious, but good communication was mentioned so often, that we decided to include a chapter to highlight the good practices we came across.

When nannies were asked what they look for in an ideal job, good communication and respect from their employers were among their top priorities. When asked what advice they would give someone about to start her first nanny job, the most common suggestion was to communicate well with your employer and to be honest. When employers of nannies were asked what advice they would give other employers, the second most important thing was communication. This emphasis on the importance of good communication was repeated in the questionnaires from au pairs and their host families.

Successfully employing a nanny or hosting an au pair is all about developing positive relationships and discussing difficulties openly and constructively before they become a real problem. Through the survey we came across many useful ideas for improving communication and they are included in this chapter, together with some of the techniques we have found to work best.

GETTING IT RIGHT FROM THE START

To communicate successfully, each party needs to feel that she is being treated with respect. You will only be able to give the impression that you respect your nanny or au pair if this is actually true. If you can't respect her, reflect on the reasons why, and decide whether you need to do anything about it.

The first few days are important as you begin to develop your relationship. Take the time to talk with and listen to your nanny or au pair, to find out how the day or the week has gone.

Be open and honest from the start. It is good to begin the relationship as you mean to go on and to express the things you are pleased about and your concerns. You should encourage your nanny or au pair to do the same. If problems are raised immediately in a constructive and helpful way, they can be dealt with before they become real issues for either of you. Both employers and nannies in our survey overwhelmingly agreed with this sentiment.

SEEING IT FROM HER POINT OF VIEW

Communication is all about perception. Your words can be interpreted differently, depending on the tone and expression you use and the state of mind of the person for whom they are intended. If your nanny or au pair lacks self-confidence, for example, she might interpret everything you say as criticism, even when it is not intended as such.

We all interpret what we hear and see according to what has happened to us in the past, how we are feeling at the moment, and our beliefs about ourselves and the world around us. On a 'bad day' we notice bad things. When we are feeling cheerful, we often don't notice the bad things, or we even see the good in them.

The only way to be sure that something you say has been interpreted as you meant it, is to check. You can do this by asking your nanny how she feels about what you've said, or by observing what she does subsequently. There are few rights and wrongs here; for the person on the receiving end, what they perceive is true for them.

Think carefully before you say something important or sensitive. Imagine you are your nanny and listen from her point of view to what you are going to say – it might help you to modify your approach so that it is more effective. This isn't about being soft, but it is about being respectful and skilful in how you communicate. It is sometimes helpful to imagine that there is an independent third party listening to the conversation and to think about how they will perceive what you say. How objective do you sound? Are you being fair? Is there another point of view?

Remember, too, that many nannies are professionally trained and have looked after other children. They may well have a useful perspective about an issue that is worrying you. Nothing pleases a nanny more than to feel her opinion is valued by you and you may well find that it is useful too.

An interesting and important observation from the survey results is that nannies and au pairs always perceived that their employers communicated with them less than their employers thought they did.

The message is simple, communicate with care and do it often.

COMMUNICATING ON A DAILY BASIS

In the survey 67 per cent of employers said that they made a point of talking to their nanny about the children and the job every day; 22 per cent said a few times a week and 11 per cent said at least once a week. For host families of au pairs the percentage was less, perhaps because the arrangement is a little less formal and the mother is around more. However, 45 per cent said that they discussed the children and the position with their au pair every day, 35 per cent said a few times a week and 20 per cent said at least once a week.

A great deal of importance is placed on regular communication. The following ideas about how you might do it, and what to cover, apply mainly to nannies whom you are leaving in sole charge of your child, but many can also be applied to au pairs.

Morning handover

Things you might like to cover include:

- General greeting/welcome. Don't underestimate the importance of this. It sounds obvious, but a number of nannies complained about not being welcomed or properly acknowledged in the mornings.
- How the children slept, and their general health that morning (e.g., tummy ache in the night, runny noses).
- Where the nanny is going that day. Have you got her contact number?
- Where you are going and when you'll be back; and contact numbers for you.
- Reminders of any key events/appointments during the day.

Evening handover

Things to cover might be:

- Any difficulties your nanny has faced during the day and how she might avoid them/deal with them if they reoccur.
- How the children have eaten.
- Anything of note which has happened during the day.
- Messages/letters from nursery or school.
- Any unusual/amusing/difficult behaviour.
- How your nanny feels about the day.

Keeping a diary

You might like to ask your nanny to keep a diary of events, in case you don't get the chance to talk to her fully before she finishes for the day. Trained nannies will be used to this idea and often take pride in doing it, particularly those who look after babies. They will keep detailed accounts of food, nappy changes, sleeps, activities, etc. Some employers in our survey suggested a diary which both parties contribute to, so that messages can easily be passed on.

Other employers prefer to be told verbally. If you aren't

interested in a diary, don't ask for one to be kept, as it could be demotivating to your nanny if you don't read it.

What to do if you are away

Sometimes you might not see your nanny in the morning or evening. It is important that she still feels you are interested in her activities. Nannies like to be independent, but a big turn-off for many of them is an employer who doesn't care about them, or about what they have been doing with the children.

A quick phone call at the start or end of your nanny's day will be appreciated. You might like to ring during the day just to check on progress, particularly if you know that she is going to have a tough day (first visit to a new play group, first day of the school holidays, etc.). You could ask her to e-mail you to let you know what she has been up to, or ask her to keep a diary.

If you have been away for a few days, it is important to have a face-to-face discussion with your nanny when you return so that you can update each other and share any issues and concerns.

HOLDING MORE FORMAL REVIEWS

As well as having frequent informal discussions with your nanny or au pair, it is helpful to sit down together, away from the children, and take time to review how things are going on a slightly more formal basis. It gives both of you the chance to raise issues or concerns that may have arisen. It can be helpful to do this more often at the start – perhaps every week to begin with, and then every month or every quarter.

Many employers of nannies in our survey used this mechanism and found it helpful. Thirty-seven per cent said they held formal reviews with their nanny at least every six months and 52 per cent of host families said they gave regular feedback to their au pairs about how they were doing.

Our experience of holding reviews with our nannies is that it is always a useful process.

Why hold a formal review?

There are six good reasons for having a regular, more formal review, even if it takes only ten minutes.

1 If everything is going well, it gives you a chance to say so. This is really appreciated by nannies and au pairs.
2 Things may be going well from your point of view, but your nanny or au pair may not be entirely happy. Setting aside a time to talk gives her the opportunity to discuss anything she might be worried about, before it becomes a problem.
3 It may be that you feel your nanny or au pair can improve in certain areas. Perhaps you feel that she isn't taking the children out enough, or that you would like her to see less of her own nanny friends during the week. Whatever the issue, setting aside time to talk on a regular basis ensures that you resolve problems before they become too serious. It also provides an opportunity to discuss issues in an objective and constructive way, rather than reacting in the heat of the moment.
4 Even if you are very happy with your nanny or au pair, and she with you, there are always things that could be done better. You might want to ask her what she feels could be improved about the job. You might consider involving the children in the discussion by asking them what else they would like to do.
5 It allows you time to think ahead and to begin to plan and discuss issues such as potty training and starting nursery or school. Involving your nanny in thinking through these more significant events will please her and could well be a help to you, too.
6 Just finding the time to talk, and being willing to listen, indicates to your nanny or au pair that you value her.

What to cover in the review

Find out what your nanny or au pair feels is going well, and what she is pleased about, and tell her what you yourself feel is going well. This is very important to her, so don't cut it short. There is always something good you can find to say about someone.

Find out, too, what she feels is not going so well, and whether anything is causing her concern or problems. Ask her, 'What are you less happy about?' or 'What do you feel you could improve on?' or 'Have you got any concerns at all about any part of the role?' And tell her about any concerns you have, and any changes you would like to see.

Ask her to give you feedback: 'What can I do to make your job easier?' or 'Is there anything you would like to change about me/us as your employers/host family?'

Let her know about any changes there will be in her role over the coming months.

Finish by summarising any actions you have agreed to take.

Some employers and host families suggested holding the review in a neutral place such as a park or café. Your nanny or au pair may express her views more openly on neutral ground.

When you go into a review, be as flexible as you can. You will get more out of your nanny or au pair if you go in with an open mind, respect her views and incorporate her ideas where possible.

GIVING FEEDBACK TO IMPROVE PERFORMANCE

In almost every relationship there will be something you are not happy about. In our survey only 20 per cent of employers (and 18 per cent of host families) said there was nothing significant that they would change about their nanny or au pair. However, most of them had small criticisms such as 'She could be more inventive with her cooking', 'She could wash the baby's bottles better', or 'I wish she was tidy and a bit more organised about the house'.

Giving feedback is an important part of developing any relationship. You really can't expect someone from outside your family to come in and begin to manage the children as you would, without giving them some clues as to what they are doing well and what you'd like done differently.

Feedback does not have to be critical. One very effective way of improving performance is to praise your nanny when she does something well. In doing so, you will almost certainly encourage her to do more of whatever it is. If you would like her to have more fun with the children, for example, when you hear them having a laugh or a cushion fight mention it afterwards: 'You know, it really makes me happy when I hear the children having such a good time with you.' Sometimes positive feedback is all that is required.

However, at other times you may need to be more direct or critical. Most of us don't enjoy criticising others and find it quite hard to do. However, it is possible to get your point across without being hurtful.

The seven steps to giving good feedback, together with some examples of real situations, are shown below. Follow these and you won't go far wrong.

THE 7 STEPS TO GIVING EFFECTIVE FEEDBACK

Steps	Poor feedback	Good feedback
1 Is the feedback really necessary? Can you put up with the problem, or are you using the opportunity to get something off your chest?	*Constant picking up on issues which are not that important.*	*Specific, appropriate discussion about important issues, both positive and negative.*
2 Be specific and give examples. Poor feedback is often too general, leaving your nanny unsure about what it is you want her to change.	*'You're not what I expected you would be.'*	*'I would prefer you to spend more time on a one-to-one basis with the children and less time meeting other nannies.'*
	'I'm disappointed in you.'	*'I feel disappointed that you don't seem to have much fun with the children.'*

Steps	Poor feedback	Good feedback
3 Give specific praise as well as criticism.	*'You are doing a good job.'*	*'I really like the way you spend time reading with the children.'*
Let your nanny or au pair know precisely what it is you are pleased about – so that she can do it again!	*'We're pleased with you.'*	*'Thank you for cooking buns with the children yesterday – they didn't stop talking about it all night!'*
4 Focus on the facts. Poor feedback can feel accusing or even insulting to the recipient. Describe the behaviour you want to change, rather than criticising her or judging her personality.	*'You're lazy.'*	*'I'm unhappy about how untidy the house is at the end of the day.'*
	'You don't care.'	*'It really is important to me that the children's clothes look smart, and I'm worried that sometimes they aren't ironed properly.'*
	'You disregard my feelings.'	*'When you come back later than you said you would, it really worries me.'*
	'James doesn't like you.'	*'James seems to me to be unsettled at the moment. How does he appear in the day time when he's with you?'*

Steps	Poor feedback	Good feedback
		(Note the use of 'I' statements, e.g., 'I feel that' rather than the more accusing 'you are'. Using 'I' helps you to sound less judgemental, while not diminishing the message.)
5 Explore alternatives, rather than telling her what to do. Involve her in finding a solution.	*'I think you should set your alarm clock earlier in the mornings.'*	*'It causes big problems when you're late. How can you make sure it doesn't happen again?'*
	'You must take the children to the park more often.'	*'I feel unhappy that the children aren't getting enough exercise. What activity would you like to do with them?'*
6 Don't overload her with feedback.	*'You are late too often, you don't take the children to the park enough, you spend too much time with other nannies, you are untidy and you don't have enough fun.'*	*Just one or two things at a time are all that any of us can handle. Try to pick the most important area and focus on it until it improves. Then move on to the next.*

Steps	Poor feedback	Good feedback
7 Finish on a constructive note, having agreed to do something different.	*'So don't forget again, will you?'*	*'So what I'm going to do is write a checklist of everything the children need to take to school on each day of the week, and you will check it each morning before you leave.'*

When you give feedback, it is best to do it somewhere private – and never in front of the children, as it can undermine your nanny or au pair's authority. Prepare for what you are going to say, especially if the subject is tricky or sensitive.

If there are a lot of areas you wish to improve, tackle them in sequence. Choose the most important and focus on that for a month or two. Then, when it has improved, move on to the next area, remembering to give positive feedback as you go. Just giving feedback may not be sufficient. A nanny who is not very good at organising her day does need to be told so, but she may also need some help from you in how to go about it (see Chapter 7).

Be prepared to compromise. How serious is the problem? Can you live with it? Some of the nannies we surveyed said they were criticised for minor things (such as hanging the dishcloth over the tap, or cutting the children's nails instead of filing them). Understandably, they found this sort of feedback irritating and de-motivating. Flexibility is key. One employer said, 'I don't have dislikes about her. She is a human being, and so has failings, but they are balanced by her good qualities.'

Finally, remember that you are not perfect, either! Ask your nanny or au pair for feedback on how she feels about you. Hopefully you'll be pleasantly surprised. She may have suggestions which will help to improve your working relationship. Two useful questions for eliciting feedback are 'What do I do that you'd like me to continue doing?' and 'What would you like me to do differently?'

Nanny perspective: In the dark

'I began work in the October, and after four weeks I had no idea what my employer thought of me. I felt I was doing a good job but was unsure. Then one day I forgot to pass a message on, and the next day I forgot to buy some nappies. I felt very cross with myself and worried that my employer would think I was incompetent.

'I was so worried that it began to affect me. The next day I forgot to take Alice's dinner money into school. That night when I told my employer, she was cross and I burst into tears. I told her I was worried that she'd think I was hopeless. She said that they were delighted with me and thought that I was the most organised nanny they had ever had.

'I was fine after that and haven't forgotten anything since. I realise now that I was in such a pickle about it all, that it was making me worse.'

Employer perspective: Softly, softly

'Our new nanny was younger than the other nannies we had employed. She was enthusiastic and the children had taken to her well. However, we were unhappy about quite a few things. After a month I drew up a list of the things I liked and the things I didn't. Although the negative list was much longer, on balance we felt that we wanted to try to keep her as the children were responding to her so well and seemed so happy.

'We decided to have weekly reviews and at the end of each week I would praise her for all the things she had done well. I tried to use praise rather than criticism where possible. So, when she took the children swimming one day without any prompting from me, I praised her and asked if it would be possible for her to do that more often – say, once a week.

'I introduced one thing at a time and sometimes I had to be more direct, for example when she started using the telephone excessively.

'It is now six months on. Things still aren't perfect, but they are vastly improved and we feel much happier. It's been a bit of a slog, but the children love her and so, I tell myself, it's all been worthwhile.'

DEALING WITH CONFLICT

No matter how skilful and well-intentioned we are, at some time we will probably have to face conflict with our nanny or au pair. Indeed, a little conflict, if dealt with well, can actually improve the relationship. Conflict does not necessarily mean a shouting match or tears – there are other, more subtle ways in which negative feelings can manifest themselves. Silence, unwillingness to talk to you, disinterest, over-compliance, arrogance and sarcasm are all indications that something is wrong.

Few people enjoy being unhappy. Whatever the cause of the conflict, and whatever the rights or wrongs of the situation, we believe that people are doing the best they can at any one time with the situation they find themselves in. How you choose to handle the moment will have a significant impact on your nanny or au pair's feelings and on the way she chooses to behave in the future.

A nanny is often extremely good at being professional and protecting the children from any negative feelings she has towards you. In the long term, though, unresolved problems will inevitably affect her morale and how well she does her job. Similarly, if you don't confront your nanny or au pair with any strong feelings you have, resentment can build up. This won't do either of you – or the children – any good.

Confronting the issues can be hard, but you may find the following tips helpful.

First of all, encourage your nanny or au pair to be honest with you, by saying things like 'You seem unhappy at the moment and

I wonder if you'd like to tell me about it' or 'You sounded angry yesterday when you left.'

Let her talk. If she's hesitant at first, don't be afraid of silence. Ask questions to find out more if you can, and let her get whatever it is off her chest. Show her you are listening, perhaps by repeating what she has said: 'So you feel frustrated that I don't let you have enough freedom?' Try not to feel or to be defensive and don't be tempted to offer solutions at this stage – it is too soon.

Once the issue is out in the open, you can begin to ask more questions to find what is the real cause of the problem. Apparent anger with you about something you said, may really be resentment about a pay increase or because she is feeling homesick. Sometimes the initial issue may just be the final straw and the real issue may lie deeper. Be willing to say you are sorry, if it's appropriate.

Once you are both satisfied that you know the cause of the problem, you can work together to find ways to solve or improve it. Try to encourage your nanny or au pair to think of the solutions or improvements herself, but help her out if she needs you to.

Conclude with a clear plan or agreement to do something different. It can be helpful to ask your nanny or au pair to summarise what you've agreed. That way you can check that you have the same understanding of what will happen next.

One useful technique, if you simply can't agree on something, is to take the issue up to a more general level until you find common ground on which you can agree. This can sometimes be enough to release the tension and help you to move forward, as in the following example.

Host-family perspective: No way out?

'Lara, our au pair, had seemed unhappy for a few weeks. I wondered whether she was homesick. Eventually it began to affect her work and she started to turn up in the morning late and bleary-eyed. When I confronted her about it, she surprised me. She said she was angry with me, as I seemed to be asking her to do too much. In her last position, she said, she didn't have to do half as much. Actually, I thought she was getting off quite lightly – she was doing well under twenty-five hours a week. If anything, I felt she should be doing more. It seemed that we had nowhere to go, as we had directly opposing views. The conversation finished without us being any closer to a solution.

'Later, when I talked to a friend about it, she gave me an idea. I sat down with Lara again and asked her what her view of an au pair's role should be. She said light household duties and helping to look after the children. I agreed with that. I asked her how she thought she could best help us in this house with those two things. She said that she liked to help with the children and that she enjoyed walking them to school in the mornings, but she hated taking the dog with her. She said she was happy dusting and vacuuming, but that she hated doing the ironing.

'So we did a deal. We agreed she would stop taking the dog to school and she would only iron the children's clothes. We agreed more formally, however, what hours she would work each day – and as a result I ended up with slightly more of her time than before. By taking a step back and agreeing what she was there to do, it enabled us to see a way through the problem.'

Common areas of conflict and ways of dealing with them

If your nanny or au pair is very assertive, and has a clear point of view with which you disagree, dismissing it with 'You're wrong' or 'That's stupid' won't help. Show that you take her seriously. Try saying, for example, 'I'm afraid I feel quite differently. Let's start at the basics and see what we can agree on.'

If a nanny or au pair says she can't or won't do something, and you suspect that it is because she lacks confidence, don't just say, 'Of course you can.' Instead encourage her: 'Well, imagine for a moment that you could do it. What would that be like?' or 'Don't worry. It took me a while to master it' or 'What is stopping you from having a go?'

If you need to suggest a particular course of action without seeming too pushy, avoid saying, 'I think you should do it like this' or 'Our last nanny did it like this.' Better to say, 'One way of doing it might be . . .' or 'Have you thought about . . . ?' or 'I'm sure you'll find your own way of sorting this, but you might like to think about . . .'

When confronted by your nanny or au pair with an accusation such as 'You don't think about me and how I feel,' it isn't enough to say, 'Yes I do'. Try asking, 'How do you know that?' or 'Has there ever been a time when you feel that I have been thoughtful?' or 'How would I be different if you thought I did consider your feelings?' and ask her to give you some examples.

It is always a good idea to ask her for her view first. The situation below, described by one employer in our survey, shows that holding your tongue sometimes pays off.

Employer perspective: Underlying problems

'Julie had worked for us as a live-in nanny for two years. We were pleased with her work and had not had any real problems before. Then, over a period of a month, I noticed that she was becoming forgetful and careless. She had twice forgotten to take our eldest child's PE kit to school; she had begun to be a little untidy and seemed not to be her usual energetic self. Then one day she forgot to pick up Rachel, our six-year-old, from a friend's house as had been agreed. I received a call at work from my friend and had to ring Julie to ask her to go and fetch Rachel.

'I felt angry and decided to have it out with Julie when I got home. To make matters worse, when I did arrive home, Julie didn't refer to the incident at all – seeming to have forgotten that it had happened. I was furious.

'Fortunately, however, I managed to start by asking Julie for her view of events. Later, I was grateful that I had taken such a considered approach. It emerged that Julie's father had been diagnosed with a serious illness. Julie was upset about it and didn't know what to do or how to deal with it.

'Julie agreed that she had been making mistakes recently. She was as unhappy about this as I was, as she loved her job. So we agreed that she would have some time off to go and see her father. Just talking about the problem seemed to help and, although it took time for things to improve, I felt more able to discuss problems and to tackle them as they arose.

'I think our relationship improved because we worked through it together. I wasn't soft on Julie but I did compromise – for the long-term good, I think.'

For more information on how to deal with conflict which might escalate into something more serious, such as gross misconduct, see Chapter 10.

REASSURING YOURSELF

Most of us will have a good feel within a few weeks of whether our nanny or au pair is meeting our needs. We will know if the house is being kept as we want, we will observe her activities with the children, and we will be able to see whether the children are happy with her. However, for many of us, an element of irrational fear still exists and it relates to the less tangible areas of child care, particularly when we are absent. 'How does she deal with tantrums when I'm not there?' 'What happens when she's tired and fed up and so are the children?' 'How much television do they really watch?' And so on.

Our concerns can be fuelled by horror stories in the press and it is sometimes tempting to consider extreme solutions such as installing video/surveillance equipment. Our view is that this is not necessary and that doing so would seriously undermine your relationship. One of the key themes for nannies in the survey was the importance of being trusted by their employer. If you can't trust your nanny or your au pair, you need to think seriously about ending your relationship with them.

There are many ways of assessing how your nanny or au pair is doing without taking such drastic action. Here are a few of them.

- Observe your children – you know them best. Notice and assess any changes in their behaviour. Look for mood swings, withdrawal, bed wetting, sudden phobias or fears, and bruises in unlikely places (e.g., back, upper arms, neck). Ask your nanny or au pair about any concerns you have.
- If your children are old enough, talk with them. Try not to ask direct questions. It is better to ask, 'What sort of day did you have today? How much did you enjoy it?' than 'Did Sarah shout at you?'
- Observe your children's reaction when the nanny or au pair appears in the morning. How enthusiastic are they?
- Observe the body language that takes place between the nanny or au pair and your children. How much spontaneous affection is there? How many smiles?
- You may want to pop home occasionally unannounced to check on proceedings. We don't recommend this as a regular habit, as your nanny might feel that you're spying on her. However, as a precaution if you are particularly concerned about something, or in the first few weeks of a nanny joining you, it may be a good idea.
- Develop good relationships with other mums in the area. If people who know you see an incident between your nanny or au pair and your children, they are likely to tell you about it. Again, be careful: none of us wishes to make our nanny or au pair feel too closely observed.

If you do have areas of concern, deal with the situation immediately. If it can't be resolved, find someone else.

SUMMARY

- Respect your nanny or au pair, both as a person and for what she brings to your family.
- Communication is based on perception, as well as fact. Check that you understand one another and deal quickly with any confusion and misunderstanding.
- Talk to your nanny or au pair about the children every day if you can – and hold regular reviews in which you talk about how she is doing and how she feels about her role.
- Give praise when you can and constructive criticism when it is needed.
- Be flexible in your approach. Ask for her ideas and be prepared to compromise when you can.
- Deal with any unhappiness quickly. Confront issues openly, and resolve them together.

7 Managing and Motivating Your Nanny or Au Pair

'She is always cheerful and nice with us.' – Child

'I feel stretched but enjoy the responsibility and the freedom.' – Nanny

'The parents have a great interest in me, which makes me want to do my best.' – Nanny

'Being an au pair is not my goal, but I'm motivated because I can improve my English and my family is very nice and friendly.' – Au pair

In our survey, 71 per cent of nannies and 75 per cent of au pairs said they felt they were being managed well. Good 'management' of your nanny or au pair is about respect, appreciation, support, trust, responsibility, challenge and fairness.

WHAT MOTIVATES NANNIES AND AU PAIRS IN GENERAL

As employers or host families we want our nannies and au pairs to be caring, happy, cheerful, conscientious, reliable, energetic, flexible, honest and willing to use their initiative. Phew! When was the last time we felt or behaved like that at work or at home?

If we want our nannies and au pairs to approach this ideal, we need to create a working environment that makes it possible for them. Working relationships are two-sided and we believe that you will get out what you put in.

What happy, motivated nannies and au pairs say

'I have never lost my enthusiasm as I have such good feedback and support from my employers all of the time.'

'I feel appreciated – my employer gives me a lot of praise so I am always willing to help as my efforts are recognised.'

'My ideas are welcomed and encouraged and I am trusted, so it makes me feel happy and motivated.'

'My boss is encouraging me to pursue a career in interior design when I'm no longer needed as a nanny here.'

'I live with an easy-going family and they trust me. They encourage me in my private life as well as my education.'

'One of the children is handicapped and I spend a lot of time doing things to help him. It has motivated me to have developmental goals to reach.'

'I have a challenging job looking after four children and I also go to college. I feel stretched, but enjoy it.'

'He does his best to please me. He recently gave me a cash bonus and when I work long hours one day, he tries to reduce them the next.'

'I have a friendly family and happy children.'

What less happy nannies and au pairs say

'I used to be very motivated, but lately he has treated me with no respect and I have to work very long hours, so I can't be bothered any more.'

'The mother frequently arranges the day. There's no point organising anything as it hardly ever gets to go ahead.'

'I am bored – the job doesn't allow me to use the qualities I know I can give. I think the parents need to relax and let me do my job.'

'I adore my charges, but I don't find the job very stimulating and any efforts seem to be taken for granted.'

'It's coming to the end of my contract and my employer doesn't feel the need to look after me now.'

'I tend to get stuck in the house all day as there are so many chores to do.'

'I'm not happy because the dad always overrules what I say.'

In our survey, we asked nannies and au pairs how motivated they felt and why. The results were remarkably consistent. Around 70 per cent of both nannies and au pairs felt motivated, about 10 per cent felt de-motivated and about 20 per cent felt neither one way nor the other. The parents' attitude had a significant impact on how motivated they felt.

NANNIES AND AU PAIRS WHO FELT MOTIVATED

Reasons for motivation	% of motivated nannies	% of motivated au pairs
Reasons to do with the nanny or au pair herself, such as 'I just love children,' 'I can always find new things to do,' 'New job, new area, lots to discover,' 'I'm happy. My life is going very well.'	42	18
Feeling appreciated, supported and trusted by the parents	35	41
Well behaved and/or lovely children	13	—
New baby on the way	5	—
Family helping me to improve my English (for au pairs)	—	23
Making new friends (for au pairs)	—	18
Other reasons (pay, shorter hours, feeling secure, new to the job)	5	—

Of those nannies who felt unhappy and de-motivated, most gave reasons relating to the way their employers were managing them, such as lack of respect, being taken for granted, not being given enough freedom, too much criticism, and not enough challenge. Au pairs gave similar answers, although they also gave homesickness and loneliness as reasons for being unhappy.

Three interesting facts emerge from these findings.

1. Some nannies and au pairs seem naturally positive, and their motivation comes from within themselves. Finding someone who has this natural disposition will clearly be a big help.
2. Your attitude and behaviour towards your nanny or au pair will have a significant effect on her feelings about her work, and on how happy she is and how motivated she feels.
3. Only a tiny minority – less than 1 per cent – of nannies and au pairs gave pay as a reason for feeling motivated or de-motivated (although it may, of course, form a part of people's feelings about being valued, cared about and treated fairly).

FINDING OUT WHAT MOTIVATES YOUR NANNY OR AU PAIR

While clear themes emerge from the research, it is also apparent that the priority a nanny or au pair gives to a particular issue will vary. The important thing is to find out what makes your nanny or au pair 'tick' and not to assume that what motivates you will motivate her.

The simplest way to do this is to ask her – an ideal time is during your regular reviews. Ask about the best and the most difficult aspects of the role and what she would most like to change. Once you've got some ideas, observe her reaction to different things you try.

Employer perspectives

'I work from home and need cover for a number of hours a day. Sometimes it doesn't matter to me whether those hours are early or later in the day, so I ask my nanny what hours she would prefer to work when I am able to choose. It makes her happy, and it doesn't really matter to me.'

****

'I find it's better to ask my nanny to work slightly longer hours and then let her finish a bit early, rather than constantly keeping her a few minutes late. I try to always stay in "credit" with the hours I pay her for.'

Note: In sharp contrast, one nanny in our survey said her employer had recently told her she 'owed' them six days' work, from times when they had allowed her to go home early over the previous year!

Nanny and au pair perspectives

'I support my home-town football team and it means a lot to me that my employers allow me time off to go to watch the matches, even when it makes their arrangements difficult.'

****

'My boss often lets me start later on a Monday morning and finish early on a Friday. I love this – and I really appreciate the effort she makes.'

****

'Every so often the children bring me a bunch of flowers. It really makes me feel appreciated.'

The most important thing is to learn what pleases your nanny or au pair and to do it whenever you can.

MANAGING AND GIVING RESPONSIBILITY

We asked nannies and their employers, au pairs and their host families how well they thought they were being managed or were managing.

Obviously people have different interpretations of what the word 'managing' means, and employers and host families generally think they are better at it than their au pairs and nannies do! However, the results were encouraging.

HOW WELL NANNIES AND AU PAIRS ARE MANAGED

Questions	Responses		
	Very well	*Well*	*Total*
Nannies: How well are you managed?	45%	26%	71%
Employers of nannies: How well do you manage your nanny?	70%	27%	97%
Au pairs: How well are you managed?	25%	50%	75%
Host families: How well do you manage your au pair?	55%	31%	86%

So how do you manage your nanny or au pair well? Much of it is to do with communicating effectively, as we have already seen. However, there are different styles of managing, which are more or less suited to different nannies and to different situations. The key, as in many things, is to be flexible.

Two distinct styles of managing your nanny or au pair are to delegate (the 'leave them to it' style), or to direct (the 'tell them how to do it' style). Which one you choose to use will depend on your nanny or au pair's personality and skills, together with the particular task or situation she faces.

Some nannies need and like clear direction. Others want to be given some basic guidelines and allowed to get on with it. However, even the latter may need direction at times, for example, when a normally confident nanny is facing potty training for the first time. The key is to ensure that you use the right style at the right time.

The delegating style is suitable when your nanny or au pair is confident and experienced, when she wants the opportunity to have a go on her own, and when you feel comfortable with her skills and willing to let go. Bear in mind, though, that excessive use of this style can lead to important things not being completed how you would like them to be, or to your nanny or au pair feeling that you don't care.

The directing style is more suitable if your nanny or au pair lacks confidence and needs your support, when she faces a new task for the first time, or when you need to feel in control. However, excessive use of this style may make your nanny feel frustrated that you don't trust her enough to make her own decisions; or it can lead to her becoming over-reliant on you and therefore not developing or improving.

Employer perspective: Lack of initiative?
'We had one nanny for several years who was competent and confident. We were happy to let her get on and manage things in her own way, with just the occasional steer. When she left us to go to college, we were very sad but our new nanny settled in well and life began to return to normal.

'However I began to feel that she was not doing enough activities with the children and seemed content to stay in the house most days. When I suggested doing things – like swimming or expeditions to the park – she would happily follow them through, but she didn't seem to use her own initiative.

'Then it struck me one day that I was managing her as I had managed our previous nanny. Perhaps she needed more direction? Being directive – or "bossy", as I think of it – is not my natural style and I felt a bit uncomfortable at first. However, it turned out I was right. I told her I would like the children to do more and I sat down with her to work out a weekly schedule – swimming on a Monday, walk on a Tuesday or Wednesday, visit to the library on Thursday, etc.

'The following week – and ever since – has been perfect. It seems this particular nanny needed me to do that for her, whereas my previous nanny would have been offended by my interference. Well, you live and learn.'

Although in the previous case study the employer needed to be more directive in order to get the best out of her nanny, our survey suggests that tension in nanny–employer relationships is more likely to arise when the nanny wants more freedom than her employer feels comfortable with. When we asked nannies what their ideal job would be, having sole charge of the children and being free to plan their own time were high on the list.

Clearly, you must be comfortable with the degree of freedom you give to your nanny or au pair, however some guidelines on how to delegate effectively may be helpful.

Delegating with confidence

Good delegation is about describing the outcome or goal that you want to achieve, but allowing your nanny or au pair to choose the method of achieving it. For example, you might say, 'I would like you to hear Charlie read every day,' but allow her to decide when and how. You might say, 'I'd like the children to get some exercise at least three times a week,' but allow her to choose what type of exercise and when she will do it. This way you don't confuse the goals with the method.

You might go a step further and ask her to help you set the goal. 'I'd like the children to have regular exercise. How many times a week do you feel they need it?'

Delegation: common obstacles and excuses

We may be reluctant to delegate for a number of reasons. We may feel that our nanny or au pair won't do something as well as we would ('She might not be very good at helping him with his homework'). Conversely, we may be worried that she'll do it better ('The children might have more fun with her than with me'). We may miss doing certain things ('But I really enjoy bathtimes'), or worry that we'll lose control ('If I let her plan the meals, I won't be sure they are getting a balanced diet'). Or we may worry about things going wrong – one employer in our survey wouldn't allow her nanny to drive the children anywhere, in case she crashed the car.

Rules of delegation

The following guidelines will help to ease these concerns and enable you to delegate effectively.

- Be clear about what you want her to achieve, and take time to explain it. For example, tell her that you'd like the children to have two portions of fruit and three portions of vegetables every day.
- Be clear about timescales: 'I'd like you to take George swimming once a week.'
- Allow her to decide how to carry out the task, but help her if she asks you to.
- Provide appropriate resources, such as paints, paper or cash.
- Monitor her progress but don't interfere unless you really have to (be prepared to allow her to make mistakes at first).
- Give constructive feedback, support her and help her to learn.
- Praise her when she does well.

Leave her some money

It is important to leave your nanny or au pair with some money each week so that she can cover the costs of activities (playgroups, swimming, etc.), and incidental purchases such as nappies and sweets. Some families don't like to leave money for treats but this can be a little short-sighted. If you don't leave your nanny or au pair enough money, you will restrict what she can do and this may demotivate her.

Many employers and host families leave a kitty which they replenish each week. It is quite reasonable to ask your nanny or au pair to keep a record of her expenses – particularly at the start of her time with you – although many employers and host families do not bother with this, and trust her to spend the money appropriately.

It is normal to pay your nanny or au pair's expenses when she is doing something in connection with the children, for example, the costs of her entry to the swimming baths and her lunch afterwards. You will probably need to leave her more money during the school holidays.

RECOGNISING HER ACHIEVEMENTS

Most of us need recognition for what we do, whether at work or at home. Recognition is not the same as pay, which is what we expect for going to work. It is about feeling appreciated and needed – and perhaps a little special, too.

There are plenty of ways of recognising your nanny or au pair's achievements. Some are easy, some require more effort. Some are cheap – or even free – and others are more expensive. But whatever your budget, you can do a lot to make your nanny or au pair feel important.

One nanny, despite being poorly paid, said she loved her job because her employers really appreciated her, respected her and made her feel wanted. Another felt motivated because her employer frequently asked her opinion on issues to do with the children and involved her in family decision-making. One au pair said that it was delightful to be given a bunch of flowers and told it was 'just for being me'.

None of these things need be expensive, or even take much effort, but they show that you care and that you respect and appreciate her. It really does make a difference. Here are some ideas.

IDEAS FOR REWARDING YOUR NANNY OR AU PAIR

Cheap and easy	More cost/effort	Major cost/effort
Say thank you	Give her a half- or whole day off unexpectedly	Allow an extra week off for a holiday
Give praise for things well done	Buy her gifts on your holidays	Pay for driving lessons
Ask her for her view about things to do with the children	Give thoughtful Christmas and birthday presents	Pay for a holiday air ticket
Involve her in some of the decisions relating to the children	Give extra cash for holidays	Give presents for long service
Acknowledge that a day has been tough		

Cheap and easy	More cost/effort	Major cost/effort
Let her finish a little early	Give her gift vouchers, or perhaps vouchers for treatment at a beauty clinic	Pay for a trip home, or for relatives/friends to visit her (one host family paid for their au pair's mum's flight to the UK)
Buy her a box of her favourite chocolates or a bunch of flowers	Provide additional petrol money	Put up her friends and relatives in your home
Give her photos of the children	Give her theatre or cinema tickets	Give her a bonus at Christmas or on her birthday or the anniversary of her joining you
Round up petrol money etc. in her favour	Pay for her to have a takeaway when she is baby-sitting for you	
Write her a thank-you letter or card	Buy her clothes	
Give her pictures and cards made by the children	Take her out for a family meal/treat	
Make her a birthday cake	Take her on – or pay for – a trip to somewhere she would really like to go	
Give her gifts related to your job (one employer who worked for a cosmetic company gave her nanny free make-up samples)	Cook her food she really likes (one host family had 'Czech nights' for their au pair)	
Pander to her sometimes (one nanny said, 'It's great – the dad makes me a cuppa in the mornings')		

Whatever you do, make sure it is over and above what is expected. In our survey we asked employers if they ever gave rewards and treats to their nanny. Some said that they did, in the form of time off or money for extra hours worked. This is not recognition. It is what the nanny has earned.

Nanny perspective: Feeling appreciated
'Every nanny likes to feel appreciated. We are responsible for the children in our care and always try to do the best we can for them. One way parents can recognise this is to give non-monetary rewards. They can be small gestures such as flowers after a long or difficult day at work.

'Sometimes employers can provide perks from their own jobs. For example, one licensing barrister that I worked for gave me guest tickets for the Reading Pop Festival. I had tried to buy some and couldn't, so I was pleased. This made me feel that my hard work had been recognised and that I was a part of the family.'

COACHING AND DEVELOPING HER SKILLS

Sometimes good communication and delegation are not enough. In order to develop, your nanny or au pair may need some instruction or guidance.

Developing her skills

It may be that your nanny or au pair is super in most respects but that you would like her to develop in a particular area – her cooking, for example, or her ability to organise herself and the children.

First you need to give her some constructive feedback to make her aware of the issue. Then you need to coach her, to enable her to improve.

Effective coaching

Talk to your nanny or au pair, so that she knows and accepts that she needs to develop in a particular area. Once she has accepted it, help her to plan and/or show her what to do. Be encouraging and supportive – show her that you have confidence in her ability.

Let her have a go, and make sure she knows you don't expect perfection immediately and that it's OK to get it wrong at first. Ask her how she thinks she's done and give her some feedback. And – as always – recognise her achievement.

Sometimes it is appropriate to help her to think through what she needs to do and how she might approach it. The following questions will help you to guide her thoughts.

- What are you hoping to achieve?
- How will it affect the children?
- How will you approach it?
- What will success look like? How will we measure it?
- What support do you need from me?
- What did you learn?
- What are the next steps?
- When shall we review progress?

At other times, you may need to show your nanny or au pair how to do something (for example, how to make up formula milk), and then let her have a go and give her some feedback.

Occasionally, coaching needs to be supplemented with more formal instruction. One employer in our survey had taken on an unqualified nanny but was supporting her on a day-release basis while she studied for a child-care qualification at her local college. Other employers have paid for their nannies to attend courses in first aid, life saving or advanced driving.

Employer perspective: Novice in the kitchen

'Philippa joined us as our new nanny and we were happy with her in all respects except for her cooking. She didn't seem to have any idea about putting together a balanced diet and she didn't seem to have much ability to produce appetising meals. We talked to her about it after a few weeks and she agreed that she had 'never been much good at cooking'.

'I asked her how we could help, and together we worked out a plan of campaign. My husband came home early one evening and took over with the children so that we could sit down and develop a set of weekly menus. We deliberately kept to things that were quick and easy to make, so that it wouldn't be too daunting or impractical for her, and we kept in the occasional fish fingers and chips, sandwiches and cheese on toast. As we put the menus together, we discussed the importance of fresh vegetables, balancing fat, carbohydrate, protein, etc.

'The next step was to practise a few of the menus. Over a period of a month I would come home early when I could and we would cook together – shepherd's pie, tuna bake, spaghetti bolognese, etc. Phillippa's confidence began to improve and she began to try out recipes for herself. She started to enjoy it and said her mum couldn't believe the transformation!

'A new restaurant has just opened in town, and I thought I might treat her and her mum to a meal as a way of saying well done.'

Nanny perspective: Organised chaos

'I had been working for my new family for two months, and frankly I was very unhappy. They were great people but they had four children and I had only looked after two before. Every moment seemed frantic, and I felt out of control. When my employer sat me down and asked me how I thought the job was going, it was actually quite a relief to be able to tell her how I felt. I thought she might ask me to leave, but she surprised me by saying that she found four children a challenge, too.

'She said that she had had to learn to develop ways of dealing with the frenzy. It was such a relief to hear that she didn't think I was useless – just normal. She asked me to write a big timetable with every day of the week and all the events that were happening (school times, play group, swimming lessons, ballet, tumble tots, etc.). I had fun doing this, the children helped me to decorate it, and we put it on the wall in the kitchen. Then she helped me to think about the things that I needed every day (e.g., nappy bag, school bags etc.) and we developed a system where one of us would ensure that the bags and the children's clothes for the next day were made ready the night before.

'I also told her that I felt the six- and four-year-old should be getting themselves dressed by now, and she agreed with me. So we started to work on this, too.

'It is now four months on, and it has all made a huge difference. I'm so glad I didn't give up and leave. Actually I feel quite proud of myself – managing with four of them. I'm not perfect yet, but a nanny friend recently commented that she admires me because I always seem so organised. Little does she know!'

Creating challenge for her

This is generally more relevant for nannies than for au pairs. The latter often already have many challenges to face being in a foreign country, away from home and with a new language to learn.

It may be that your nanny is excellent at everything she does and you are happy. However, in our survey we asked nannies whether they felt stretched in their current job, and whether that was important to them. A large majority (68 per cent) said they did feel stretched, and an even larger majority (74 per cent) said it was important to them.

Interestingly, when we asked employers how important they thought feeling stretched was to their nanny, they appear to have underestimated it. So talk to your nanny and find out if she wants more challenges and, if so, what appeals to her.

You can build on skills she already has and enjoys using, such as sewing, drawing, modelling or singing. Or you can create new challenges, perhaps by giving her additional responsibilities or by giving her one-off goals to meet. We've tried both, and have had some great successes.

Ideas for giving additional responsibility – ask your nanny to:

- Make cards with the children – birthdays, thank-you cards, etc.
- Help your children with their homework each evening.
- Pack the children's clothes before holidays/weekends away.
- Sort through the children's clothes and decide what they need for the summer/winter. Perhaps ask her to buy some missing items.
- Sort through the children's toys. Note what else is needed and what should be thrown away.
- Take on responsibility for developing your children's skills, such as teaching them to ride a bike or to learn the alphabet.

Ideas for one-off challenges – ask your nanny to:

- Arrange one of your children's parties for you – decorate the house, make costumes, organise games, etc.
- Involve your children in planning and decorating their bedrooms.
- Make Christmas cards and decorations with the children.
- Plan a treasure hunt for them.
- Organise an adventure such as a day's trip on the train or, for older children, a camping expedition.
- Make a model (e.g., a fort, a doll's house, a train track) with or for the children.
- Prepare a concert or a play with the children, for performance to the family or to their friends.

Asking your nanny to do something extra doesn't necessarily mean that you need to pay her more – although, depending on what she takes on, you might choose to reward her in some way.

Looking to the longer term

Au pairs are usually here with the specific aim of improving their spoken and written English skills. They may well have a long-term plan to go on to college or university when they return home.

Nannies are different in that many of them have already studied and qualified in their chosen career. However, few nannies continue being nannies over the age of thirty (in the survey 80 per cent were thirty or younger, and only 6 per cent were over thirty-five). Many go on to have their own children and may stop working altogether; and some may decide to move on to something different. You may find that you have a role to play in helping your nanny to think through what she would like to do in the longer term.

Sometimes nannies find that the challenge goes once the children go to school, and they haven't enough to do during a large part of the day. Just loading on domestic chores is unlikely to appeal, so it's worth thinking about other ways of keeping your nanny's interest if you want her to stay with you.

We asked nannies and au pairs how much they discussed their longer-term plans with their employers, and whether they felt their employers helped them with their plans. Seventy-five per cent of nannies and 86 per cent of au pairs said that their employers or host families did discuss their plans with them, and 80 per cent of nannies and 85 per cent of au pairs felt that they were helped to fulfil their plans.

Ways of helping your nanny

Employers and host families have helped their nannies and au pairs in a wide variety of ways, from which we have taken the following suggestions.

- Encourage her to talk about her plans, to think them through and to research what is available. If appropriate, help her to complete application forms.
- Ask if she would like to take up a course at college. There are many advanced courses available in child care and early-years studies. Or she may be interested in something totally different; our survey showed nannies studying for interior design, counselling, therapy, reflexology and teaching.
- Agree to extend a placement (for an au pair) so she can take higher-level English exams.

- Find some day-time voluntary work, perhaps at your child's school or with a local community group (something she could cancel in an emergency, if, for example, one of your children became ill).

There are many ways of challenging and stretching your nanny or au pair if that is what she wants. The important thing is to talk to her, find out what she would like to do, and be flexible and supportive where you can.

SUMMARY

- We expect our nannies and au pairs to be caring, happy, cheerful, conscientious, reliable, energetic, flexible, honest and willing to use their initiative. Therefore we have to create an environment that allows them to flourish in this way.
- Once your nanny is with you, how much you pay her will not be the most important factor in determining how motivated she feels. The way you manage her will have a far more significant effect on how she feels about her work.
- You have a choice of management styles – being directive or giving your nanny or au pair a free rein. Both styles can be helpful. The key is recognising when to use each one and being flexible enough to change when required.
- Showing that you respect your nanny or au pair and recognising her hard work is an important element of maintaining a good relationship. It needn't cost you much – but you do need to do it from time to time.
- All nannies and au pairs can improve what they do. You may need to spend some time coaching your nanny or au pair to help her to develop her skills.
- Many nannies relish a challenge and, if yours does, it is worth spending time planning how to provide one for her. Helping her to think about and to plan her future may increase the time she is willing to stay with you.

8 Pay, Hours and Benefits for Nannies

'If you want a superstar, you'll have to pay for one.' – Mum

'If your nanny is good, pay her well.' – Dad

When we asked nannies what they looked for in their ideal job, first on the list of their answers was good pay and benefits. It is an important area to get right, because misunderstandings can cause a great deal of resentment, even if both parties are well intentioned. It is vital to discuss and agree pay, hours and benefits with your nanny, and to review them at regular intervals to ensure that you are in line with market rates and that misunderstandings do not arise.

HOURS OF WORK

We asked nannies what they liked least about their current job. By far the most frequently mentioned issue (three times more often than anything else), was the hours.

Nanny perspective: Long hours
'I'm asked to baby-sit at the last minute (half an hour's notice) and the employers are often back late.'
'I work long hours – at weekends I'm exhausted.'
'I never leave on time.'

'They often phone at 6 pm and say they'll be late, when I'm supposed to finish at 6.30 pm.'
'Too many hours – eighty a week – and he still doesn't think that I do enough.'
'I wish the hours were as we agreed in the interview.'

Be honest right from the start about the hours you need, and you'll avoid causing the sort of resentment shown in the above comments. One employer answering our survey suggested that it's best to ask for more hours than you need, and to let your nanny finish early, than constantly to keep her late.

There are no legal restrictions on how many hours a week a nanny may work, so it is up to you to decide what it is you need, and what you can reasonably ask her to do. Live-in nannies normally work up to fifty-five hours a week (that is, five eleven-hour days), and may also be expected to baby-sit up to twice a week (during the week). Live-out nannies normally work forty-five to fifty hours a week (that is, five nine- or ten-hour days). They may be willing to baby-sit once or twice a week for extra pay, but may well have other commitments in the evenings.

Some employers need longer hours than this and if you do, be honest and specific from the start. Agree the hours with your nanny and try to stick to them. Compensate her when she does additional work, by giving her extra time off, less baby-sitting, early finishes or extra pay. If you do need very long hours, or some weekend cover, it may be worth considering employing more than one nanny or combining a nanny with an au pair or baby-sitter.

All nannies normally expect to have two days off a week. A nanny may sometimes be willing to work a regular Saturday or Sunday, providing that she has a corresponding day off in the week. Occasional weekend work may also be acceptable, providing that you pay her well or give her plenty of time off in lieu. Finding a nanny who is prepared to work regular weekends may be difficult.

Some nannies in our survey regularly worked significantly more than the hours outlined above. Those who did were understandably tired and de-motivated. A tired nanny may not be a safe or a happy one.

If you have a live-in nanny, it is important to try not to impinge on her time off. Think twice before asking her to look after the children while you just 'nip out to get some milk'. To you it may seem a small favour, but to her it may seem a big one.

If you ask your nanny not to work for the day, perhaps because you fancy taking the children off somewhere, it is usual to pay her for this time or to agree an alternative time for her to make up the hours (as long as the arrangement is in her favour). After all, if your own employer asked you not to come in for the day, you would still expect to be paid for it.

HOLIDAY ENTITLEMENT

Under the European Working Time Directive, all nannies are legally entitled to four weeks' paid holiday each year. You can count public holidays as part of this time – although many employers give them in addition and many nannies will expect this.

You can insist that she takes her holidays when you do, but the legislation says that the notice you give her should be twice the length of the leave to be taken. For example, if you are going to take a week's holiday, you need to give her at least two weeks' notice. In practice, most employers try to provide more notice than this, in order to allow their nanny to make arrangements to go away if she chooses. Some employers ask their nanny to take half her holidays when the employer does and half when she herself chooses.

Whatever you decide do, it makes sense to keep a record of the holidays your nanny takes throughout the year.

Typical questions about holidays

Q: My nanny wants to carry her holidays over and take more next year. What should I do?

A: This is very much up to you, and ideally it is something that will have been agreed in her contract. Many employers would not agree to this as a general principle, but might make an allowance for a special occasion, such as a one-off holiday of a lifetime, or her honeymoon. It may be worth doing if your nanny has a real urge to travel, otherwise you may risk losing her.

Q: I asked my nanny to work on a bank holiday and she agreed. How much should I pay her?

A: The key is to make sure this is a voluntary agreement and to reward her well. You might agree to double her pay for that day, for example (common practice would suggest that at the very least it should be time and a half). Or you might allow her to take additional time off in lieu of the time she has worked (a day and a half or two days for each bank holiday worked).

Q: My nanny has already had her contracted four weeks off this year and we are going away again. Can I ask her to come in while we are away and sort the children's toys out?

A: Again, this is an issue you should have discussed and agreed with your nanny when you took her on. If you are asking her to come in to carry out tasks that are a part of her job description, it is probably all right, as long as you handle it sensitively. However, asking her to come in to clean the house would probably not be acceptable to her.

Q: We are taking our nanny on holiday with us this year to Florida. We won't ask her to have the children all the time, and she is looking forward to going. Does this count towards her annual leave?

A: No – sorry. Even if she has a fabulous time, going away with you counts as a perk of the job, rather than as holiday time.

Q: Our nanny joined us halfway through the year. How much holiday is she entitled to?

A: You will need to work it out on a pro-rata basis. For example, if she joined you on 1 September and has four weeks' annual holiday entitlement, you would work out her remaining holiday for the year as follows. Assuming her holiday year runs from January to January (and you would state this in her contract), she has four months left – or one-third of the year. If you multiply this by her total entitlement (four weeks), you get the number of weeks she has left to take. For someone who does a five-day week, the sum would be $\frac{4}{12} \times 4 = 1.33$ weeks (or a week and two days, when rounded up).

Q: Our nanny works part-time. How do I work out her holiday entitlement?

A: If she works part-time and you need to pro-rata her holidays, it is sensible to do it in days rather than weeks. If she works a three-day week and joined you on 1 May with five weeks' total holiday entitlement, her yearly holiday entitlement comes to a total of fifteen days. There are eight months of the year left, so she has ten days left to take ($\frac{8}{12} \times 15 = 10$ days). The fairest way of allocating this would be to allow her three complete weeks (nine days) off, plus an extra day on a day when she would normally be working.

Q: Our nanny is leaving and hasn't taken all her holidays. What should we do?

A: First you need to work out how many days' holiday she is 'owed'. Let's say she works full-time and is entitled to four weeks' holiday. She has already taken ten days and is due to leave on 30 September. Her holiday entitlement up to 30 September is $\frac{9}{12} \times 4 = 3$ weeks. She has already taken two weeks' holiday and so she is owed one week. You can either allow her to leave a week early, or pay her for the holiday time she is owed.

Note: If your nanny is leaving partway through the year, and effectively 'owes' you some holiday, you can, if you wish, deduct the owed time from her pay or ask her to work the additional hours.

PAY RATES

The difference between net and gross pay

Nannies' salaries are often quoted as net rather than gross pay. Net pay is the amount that the nanny takes home after all deductions such as tax have been paid.

There is a considerable difference between net and gross pay. So, when discussing pay with agencies or with nannies, make sure you are clear about whether you are talking net or gross salary. And if you negotiate a net salary with your nanny, bear in mind that you will have to add on the cost of her tax and National Insurance (NI) contributions. On top of this, you will have to pay employer's National Insurance contributions.

The table gives the approximate values of net and gross pay and the total cost to you, the employer (after you have also paid your employer's National Insurance contributions). The figures shown are those for a nanny with one job and a standard personal tax allowance.

APPROXIMATE VALUES OF NET PAY, GROSS PAY AND TOTAL EMPLOYMENT COST

Net pay (weekly)	Gross pay (weekly)	Total cost to employer
What the nanny receives in her pocket	*The nanny's net pay, plus her tax and NI contributions, which the employer pays for her*	*The nanny's gross pay, plus the cost of the employer's NI contributions*
£150	£177	£188
£200	£250	£271
£250	£324	£353
£300	£397	£436
£350	£471	£518
£400	£543	£599

You should check the exact figures with your local tax office, as they vary from year to year and will depend on your nanny's tax code and employment history. Your tax office will also be able to help if you need assistance to work out your nanny's gross pay from a net figure that you have agreed with her.

The minimum wage

It is a legal requirement to pay your nanny at least the national minimum wage. However, it is likely that you will be paying above this if your nanny's salary is in line with market rates. The minimum wage is an hourly rate of pay set by the government each year. A slightly lower amount applies for eighteen- to twenty-one-year-olds than for twenty-two-year-olds and older.

Currently, most live-in nannies are excluded from this legislation – that is, the minimum wage does not apply to them. However, if your nanny's accommodation is separate from yours (if, for example, she has her own flat with a separate entrance) the minimum wage does apply, but you are eligible for an allowance. This can be offset against the national minimum wage hourly rate. Your local tax office will be able to tell you what this is in any given year. (To ensure that you are paying the minimum wage, take the nanny's gross weekly or monthly pay and divide that by the number of hours she works in the given period.)

How to find out the 'going rate' for a nanny

When employing a nanny for the first time it is important to identify how much you will need to pay. Once she is with you, it is a good idea to check her level of pay every year, to see that your package is still competitive.

In order to find out what the going rate is, you can:

- Call your local nanny training college and ask to speak to one of the tutors. They will normally be happy to give you a pay range for a newly qualified nanny in your area.
- Ask friends who employ nannies what they pay and what additional benefits they offer.
- If you are using a nanny agency, they will be able to advise you.
- The Professional Association of Nursery Nurses (PANN) may be able to give you details of recent nanny salary surveys and they will be happy to answer pay-related queries.
- Ask the people you interview what they are currently earning and what they expect to earn in terms of salary and other benefits. You will soon build up a picture of what is expected.

Remember that live-in nannies are paid less than live-out nannies because the former have fewer living expenses.

We believe that you generally get what you pay for. Our advice is to check the going rates in your area and then to pay as much as you can afford within the range. It is unrealistic to pay your nanny less than the going rate and expect her to be motivated.

Employer perspective: It pays to be generous

'When we offered our nanny job to Jenny, she said that she would like to earn a little more. It wasn't much, but we felt that we had offered her enough as it was and we refused. In the end she joined us anyway and she turned out to be a great nanny.

'After she had been with us for a few months, she approached me and said that all of her nanny friends in the area were earning more than she was. She felt upset and wondered if we would be willing to increase her salary. I did a bit of research and discovered that she was right.

'We decided to meet her needs and we increased her salary to the level she had asked for originally. With hindsight, I should have done more checking to start with. For the sake of a bit of time and a few pounds, I could have avoided some hard feelings.'

Additional costs

In addition to basic pay, you should expect to pay automatically for:

- Food for the nanny while she is working for you. For live-in nannies this is a little more complex. Some employers buy all her food, others supply her core diet (dairy products, fruit, vegetables, meat and drinks) but expect her to purchase any treats.
- The expenses she incurs if, for example, she takes the children out for the day.
- If she uses her own car, petrol costs incurred during working hours (although not to and from work). You can find out

current mileage rates from any of the major motoring organisations. If the nanny uses your car in her own time, you might arrange for her to pay separately for the petrol she uses.

- If she uses her own car, the additional cost (over and above her normal insurance premium) of insuring her car to carry your children. The cost of any children's car seats etc. she needs in order to carry out her job.
- A live-in nanny will expect her own room, although she may have to share a bathroom. She will expect to have her own television. You will pay all her bills. Some families ask the nanny to contribute to the phone bill; others provide her with her own telephone line and ask her to settle her own bill.

How you pay your nanny is an important aspect to consider. Nowadays, most people arrange a standing-order payment to go straight into the nanny's account. Some employers pay weekly and others monthly. If it doesn't matter to you, ask your nanny which she would prefer.

Pay slips

However you pay your nanny, she is legally entitled to a regular pay slip which shows her gross and net pay and how much the tax and National Insurance comes to. It need not be complicated.

EXAMPLE PAY SLIP

Monthly pay slip for Sarah Stevens

Date ________

Gross monthly pay	£
Deductions:	
National Insurance contributions	£
Tax deducted	£
Net monthly pay	£

SALARY INCREASES

In our survey we asked employers how often they increased their nanny's salary. A large majority (70 per cent) said they did so once a year, 16 per cent said every they did so every six months, and 14 per cent said they never did so, or that it was not applicable.

Some employers start their nanny on a lower rate of pay so that after a certain period – perhaps three or six months – they can raise it as a way of recognising her effort and rewarding her hard work. We recommend that as a minimum you increase your nanny's salary once a year by at least the rate of inflation. Whatever you do, you should make it very clear at the start of your relationship, so there is no room for misunderstanding.

If your nanny's workload increases significantly – for example, if her hours increase, or if you have another baby – you should also increase her salary (just as we would expect our own salary to go up, if we were given additional responsibilities at work or were asked to do longer hours).

When deciding how much to increase her salary by, it is worth looking at local market rates. If you have three or more children (in our survey 65 per cent of nannies looked after only one or two), or if your circumstances are unusual or demanding, you may have to pay a premium to keep a good nanny. There are no rules here, but as a rough guide we have paid 10–15 per cent more after each new baby (although we have usually included the annual inflation increase in this payment). The only exception was when we employed a new nanny while we were pregnant, and took the extra child into consideration when agreeing the new nanny's salary.

As we have said before, see how much you can afford to pay and be as generous as you can.

BONUSES

Employers vary in what they provide and, of course, it will depend on what you can afford. You might choose to give your nanny a week's extra salary at Christmas or to give her a bonus to reward a particular job well done.

Bonuses may be given as a way of saying thank you and of rewarding your nanny without having to increase your weekly costs (but they should not replace annual salary increases). One employer gave her nanny a bonus because she had made the school holidays so much fun for the children. Another gave one to thank the nanny for being so flexible and helpful when the family was going through a particularly difficult time. Some employers give their nanny a bonus when they themselves receive a bonus or salary increase.

Be aware, however, that giving a bonus may create expectations which you cannot meet.

Nanny perspective: Taken away from me

'I had been working for my employers for six months when at Christmas they gave a bonus of a week's salary. I was delighted, as it was totally unexpected and it came at a time when I really needed it.

'However I assumed that the same thing would happen this year.

'When my employers apologised and said they couldn't afford to give me a bonus this Christmas, I felt disappointed. It left me wondering if they weren't happy with me any more.'

So, what pleases a nanny one year may cause disappointment if it doesn't happen the next year. The mistake the employer made here was not making the nature of the original bonus clear and not managing the nanny's expectations about their financial position. Perhaps they could have tried to make up for it in some other small way – extra time off over Christmas, for example.

However, it isn't all bad news. Here's a story from a nanny for whom a well-timed bonus made a big difference.

Nanny perspective: The nightmare house move

'I had been with my employer for two years and enjoyed working for them. When they decided to move house I had a big decision to make, as the journey would be considerably longer for me. In the end, I decided to go with them.

'The first two months in the new house were awful. I was struggling with a longer journey (more than I had anticipated) and everywhere was in such a mess. The house was old and nothing worked properly. I spent several days with no heating and two days with no electricity. We were still living out of boxes and I could never find anything. The situation didn't seem to be getting any better. Much as I loved the children, I was beginning to contemplate looking for another job.

'Then one day my employer came home and said that she really valued my effort, that she knew what a hard time I was having and that she was going to give me a bonus as a way of saying thank you.

'It was quite a lot – a week's salary. It didn't make the problems go away, but knowing that they appreciated the effort I was making, made them easier to put up with.'

OVERTIME

If the hours the nanny is expected to work have been clearly set out and agreed, paying for overtime is easy. You agree an hourly rate with your nanny and pay her for the extra time she spends working for you.

However, some families have a less-defined working day and expect the nanny to be flexible within certain parameters. In these cases, what counts as overtime can be unclear – and misunderstanding and resentment can creep in. Our advice is to make it as clear as possible. Agree with your nanny on the first day what will constitute overtime and what will not.

Legally, any additional pay that the nanny earns from working overtime is liable for tax and National Insurance.

TAX AND NATIONAL INSURANCE

As an employer you are legally responsible for paying your nanny's tax and National Insurance, and you need to keep a historical record of your payments and deductions for the last five years. Some employers try to avoid paying, but there are good reasons why you should pay.

- It is against the law not to, and if you are found out it is you, not your nanny, who will be liable to pay it back – plus interest and penalties.
- Failure to pay can cause your nanny serious problems. For example, she may have difficulty taking out a loan or a mortgage. It may also affect her entitlement to unemployment benefit and a state pension: the right to both is earned by payment of tax and National Insurance.
- It could be embarrassing if you get caught!
- Some employers try to get out of paying by claiming that their nannies are self-employed. However, the tax office is unlikely to view a nanny as being self-employed.

Exemption

There is one situation in which you do not have to pay tax and National Insurance. If your nanny earns below a minimum amount defined by the tax office each year, she will not be liable for tax or National Insurance. This amount is low and would probably only apply if you employed her for a very few hours each week. Your tax office will be able to tell you the current rate.

If you take on a temporary nanny, you must still pay her tax and National Insurance contributions. Probably the best way of avoiding this hassle is to use a temporary nanny from an agency. You pay the agency for her services, and they sort out her tax and National Insurance payments.

If you employ an overseas nanny, her salary will also be subject to tax and National Insurance payments and you will need to apply for a National Insurance number for her.

Ways of paying tax and National Insurance

There are two ways of paying tax and National Insurance: PAYE and the Simplified Deduction Scheme. Which you use will depend on how much your nanny earns. To find out, you can call the New Employer's Help Line (the number is in Useful Contacts).

Both schemes have written guidelines to follow and a help line should you need some assistance. The Simplified Deduction Scheme is probably the more straightforward method.

The Simplified Deduction Scheme

Call your local tax office and ask them to send you an information pack; this will include full details of the scheme.

You will need to complete a form and return it to the tax office, after which they will send you a deduction card (P12). You then use the tables provided in the information pack to work out how much tax and National Insurance has to be paid, based on your nanny's salary and her tax allowances. (If you find the tables difficult to interpret, you can ring up your local tax office who will give advice and answer your queries.) You complete the deduction card on a weekly, monthly or quarterly basis, and once a quarter you send your payment to the tax office, using the forms provided.

Once a year (in April) you have to send the completed P12 back to the tax office. You will have to include details of any other benefits your nanny receives – personal use of a car, free petrol, etc. – which may be liable for tax. The tax office will then send you a new P12, together with a new set of tables for the next financial year. You will need to calculate your nanny's pay again, even if she hasn't had an increase from you, as the change in allowances will affect it.

And that's it! Some employers make a standing-order payment from their own account into a sleeping 'nanny account' each week or month, so that when they come to pay the National Insurance and tax each quarter they have the money waiting.

We find that the process takes about half an hour every quarter, and an additional half an hour once a year.

If you have to use the PAYE scheme to pay your nanny, it will take you a little longer. If you are uncertain about what to do, your local tax office or nanny agency will help you to sort it out.

Paying someone to do it for you

If you don't want to spend time on the administration, you can pay an annual fee to a company specialising in paying nanny tax and National Insurance. Such companies advertise in local papers and parenting magazines, and your local tax office may be able to recommend one (see Useful Contacts).

There are three main advantages of using an external company. First, it saves you time and hassle. Second, the company will deal with more complex issues, such as part-time nannies who also work for other families, nanny-share arrangements, maternity and sick pay, overseas nannies, tax rebates and so on. Third, the company are there to provide advice on any other pay issues which may arise.

The disadvantage is that you have to pay them for their services!

SICK PAY AND MATERNITY PAY

Sick pay

Employers vary widely on how much paid sick leave they are prepared to give their nanny – and it is discretionary.

Some employers tell their nannies that sickness will be paid at the employer's discretion and then wait to see if they feel that the sickness is genuine or not. Others will pay their nanny up to one day's sick pay for every day of the week she works – so five days a year in total, for a full-time nanny. However, good practice would suggest that you give her two to four paid weeks a year.

All nannies are entitled to Statutory Sick Pay (SSP), except for nannies on a temporary contract of less than thirteen weeks or those who earn below the National Insurance threshold. SSP has three waiting days of consecutive absence before it kicks into action and is paid at a flat rate. The amount is fixed and it is adjusted each tax year. It is treated as pay, so you have to deduct tax and National Insurance payments from it in the normal way. You pay the money to your nanny, and most employers can claim most of it back. Your local tax or social security office will advise you about this.

If your nanny is off sick for four days or more, it is important to keep a note of the absence, together with any payments you have made. The details of sick pay, and of the records you are required to keep, are clearly explained in the guidance notes you receive from your local tax office. You can call the employers' help line for advice if necessary.

Many of us dread the day our nanny is ill. However, it is bound to happen at some time and it is worth making contingency plans for when it does.

Maternity pay

If your nanny becomes pregnant while she is working for you, she will be entitled to eighteen weeks of maternity leave, during which time you will have to pay her Statutory Maternity Pay (SMP). The good news is that you can usually claim all the money back – before you have to pay it – and you even get a little extra as compensation.

During her pregnancy, your nanny will be entitled to take reasonable paid time off for antenatal care (regardless of how long she has been with you).

It is against the law to terminate a nanny's employment simply because she is pregnant.

Detailed guidance notes are available from your tax or social security office to help you to manage the situation and there is a national help line if you need further assistance. An organisation called the Maternity Alliance also offers advice and guidance.

Managing your nanny while she is pregnant can be quite a challenge. Try asking her how she feels about the situation and how she would like you to support her throughout the pregnancy. By discussing the situation with her regularly, you will help to ensure that any issues are dealt with before they become problems.

OTHER PAY QUERIES

Nanny-share arrangements

One of the families involved in the share usually takes on the responsibility of paying the nanny and sorting out her tax and National Insurance payments, and it is this family who are liable in the event of any tax or National Insurance being unpaid. It might be wise, therefore, to have a written agreement to share the employment costs.

When a nanny works for two employers separately, but in the

same week, the tax situation can become quite complex. In this case, we suggest that you contact your tax office and discuss the options available to you and your nanny. Alternatively, you can employ a specialist company to sort this out – they may be able to save you some money.

It is worth bearing in mind that money issues are one of the most commonly cited reasons for nanny-share arrangements breaking down. It really is worth spending time with the other family to get it right, and it is worth reviewing your arrangement at regular intervals.

Proxy parenting

If you go away and leave your nanny in sole charge of the children overnight, you'll need to come to an arrangement with her, to compensate her for the additional hours she works.

There are many different ways of doing this. If your children are past the waking-up-at-night stage, it may be sufficient to pay her overtime, for example up to 11 pm and from 6.30 am in the morning up to her normal start time. Most employers also give their nanny a bonus for agreeing to help, and, if possible, time off when they return (particularly for longer periods of sole care).

However, if your children wake up during the night, you might have to consider paying your nanny more money to make it worth her while. Being on duty for twenty-four hours a day is a demanding requirement for any job.

Bringing her child to work

Sometimes a nanny continues to work once she has had her own child, and brings the child to work with her. In this case, it is usual to pay her less; but there are no set guidelines. A sensible way to think about it would be to work out how much it would cost the nanny to have her own child cared for by a child minder, and take this amount off her old pay (if she has previously worked for you), or off the going rate for a nanny. You will then have to add something back on – to ensure that you are paying enough to make it worth her while to come back to work.

Jury service

If your nanny has a summons to do jury service, it may not be easy to manage. What can you do?

Your nanny will be given between six and eight weeks' notice of the date when she has to appear in court. The courts tend to be quite lenient with employers of nannies, and usually allow your nanny to ask for a deferral. However, they will expect her to complete her jury service within six months of this date (preferably), and within a year of being asked (definitely). In extreme cases they might allow two deferrals; but no more than that. There is a legal requirement on almost everyone to complete jury service when requested.

Jury service normally lasts for two weeks (ten working days). If a trial is likely to take more than this, and some do, the nanny can ask the judge to be excused. She will have to justify why she cannot stay for longer than two weeks. The fact that you are unable to work if your nanny is on jury service is likely to be seen as a reasonable excuse.

The courts will pay your nanny's travel expenses and a small subsistence allowance. You do not have to pay her for the time she is away but most employers do, as she could be seriously out of pocket otherwise (through no fault of her own). If she applies for it, the courts will pay her a small, fixed-rate, daily income allowance, and you can claim this back from her if you wish.

Don't forget, if your nanny does have to do jury service, that it may be a stressful time for her as well as for you. Some trials can be quite unpleasant and she may find the experience an uncomfortable one.

What to do when she leaves

You must provide your nanny with a final payment, inform your tax office, complete your simplified deduction card and send off any outstanding tax and National Insurance payments. You must work out any holidays due and sort out payment arrangements with your bank if you have been paying her by direct debit.

Employers' queries about pay

TYPICAL PROBLEMS AND QUERIES ABOUT PAY

Situation	Suggestions
'My nanny complains that her nanny friends are earning more than she is. What should we do?'	• Check if her friends are local. Geography can make a difference to rates of pay. • Check with local nanny agencies to see what the going rate is, or ring the Professional Association of Nursery Nurses (PANN). If she is right, consider increasing her salary if you can afford it. Or try to improve another benefit. If she already earns a competitive wage, share your information with her and be kind but firm.
'My nanny discusses her pay and benefits with her nanny friends.'	• This is common and you can't really prevent it. • Try to provide her with rewards so that she has something to boast about.
'We can't afford to give our nanny an increase this year.'	• Be honest with your nanny and explain your reasons. • Try to provide her with other benefits, such as extra time off, if you can.
'Our nanny has been with us for five years and we find that we're paying her more than the market rate.'	• Console yourself that this is probably part of the reason why she is still with you, and that your children have had consistent care for all that time. • Remember that you have not had to pay for agency or advertising costs over the five years. • Try to provide her with other benefits, such as extra time off.

OTHER BENEFITS

Additional benefits you might wish to consider providing (and which were mentioned frequently in our survey) are:

- Use of a car/free petrol for her own personal use. Paid insurance and breakdown cover for the car.
- Free use of the telephone and/or a mobile phone.
- For a live-in nanny, the size and number/type of rooms provided for her will be a significant benefit, as will the frequency and type of holidays she takes with the family.
- Facilities in her room such as a video (most nannies will expect a television as a matter of course), mini-fridge, CD player, etc.
- Additional sick pay.
- Paid trips home (if you have a live-in nanny).
- Cost of further education (first-aid course/language lessons, etc.).
- Additional holiday time.
- Membership of a local gym, health club, swimming pool, etc.
- Extra time off.
- For live-out nannies, some employers pay travel expenses to and from work.

Note: The Inland Revenue may consider some benefits taxable. Your local tax office will advise you about this.

One of the purposes of providing benefits is to make the job more attractive to your nanny and to ensure that she feels fairly rewarded. With this in mind, you might want to ask her what benefits she would like, and agree a flexible package with her. For some nannies, membership of your gym would be a fantastic benefit; for others the mere thought might induce a panic attack.

If you can work out the approximate value of the benefits and offer her alternatives, you may well get better value for your money.

SUMMARY

- Be clear about the hours you want your nanny to work, and try to stick to them wherever possible. Reward your nanny if she has had to work longer than your agreement specifies.
- All nannies are entitled to four weeks' paid holiday a year.
- Many nannies talk about net pay rather than gross pay. It is important to distinguish between the two, as there is a significant difference.
- Try to find out the going rate for a nanny in your area, and pay it if you can. Don't forget that in addition to your nanny's salary, there will be some hidden costs.
- Think carefully about how often you will increase your nanny's salary and whether you can give her any bonuses during the year.
- You are legally responsible for paying the tax and National Insurance on your nanny's salary.
- All nannies are entitled to Statutory Sick Pay and Statutory Maternity Pay, but as an employer you can claim some, if not all, of it back.
- You can consider giving your nanny other benefits to add to her total package. They will increase the attractiveness of the job, and may help you keep her for longer.
- It is vital to clarify hours, pay and benefits with your nanny at the start of her employment, and to review the situation regularly to ensure that there is no misunderstanding.

9 Pocket Money, Hours and Benefits for Au Pairs

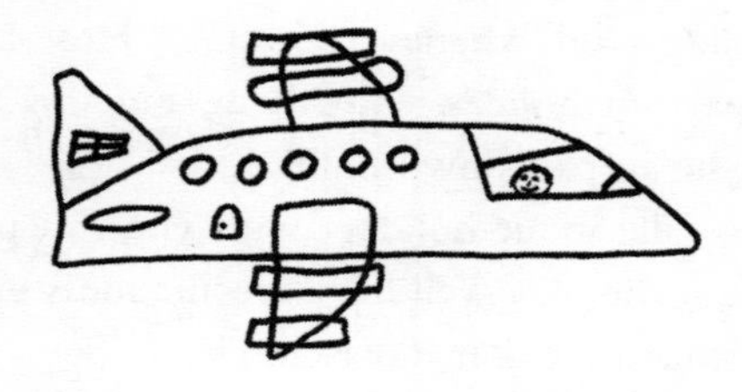

'As a treat, we paid for her flight home for Christmas.' – Dad

'My family is great – they let me use the internet, so I can e-mail my friends and family.' – Au pair

This chapter answers your most common questions relating to pocket money, hours and benefits for au pairs. It is important that you are clear right from the start about these basic elements and that you review them at the end of the first week to ensure that there are no misunderstandings.

HOURS

To recap briefly on what we said in Chapter 1, strictly speaking, the term 'au pair' applies only to people from certain non-EU countries. The Home Office sets clear guidelines about how many hours they should help in the home (e.g., up to five hours each day and a maximum of twenty-five hours each week, with two full days off; and they may baby-sit up to twice a week in return for pocket money, board and lodging). In the daytime they must have time off to attend language classes at a local college. There are no Home Office guidelines for au pairs from EU countries, but agencies usually recommend that they work similar hours. Au pairs who work under an 'au pair plus' arrangement, may work more hours a week for more pocket money.

HOLIDAY ENTITLEMENT

There are no rules here, but the general guideline seems to be one week's holiday for every six months that the au pair is with you, plus public holidays off whenever possible. Host families should take their au pair on holiday with them, but this time does not count towards the au pair's own holiday.

It is wise to talk about holidays with your au pair before she starts with you, as she may well have specific ideas or plans – to go home for Christmas or Easter, for example.

POCKET MONEY

There are three main ways of finding out how much pocket money you should pay.

The Home Office issues minimum guidelines, which you can get direct from them or from their website. If you are using an au pair agency (and most host families do), they will be able to advise you. In addition you can ask other local host families what they pay and what additional benefits they offer.

As always, it is good to pay a little more than the minimum if you want your au pair to feel good about being with you and your family.

National Insurance and tax are not payable for au pairs, as they are not employees. However, if you decided to have an 'au pair plus' arrangement with an au pair from an EU country, you may then be liable for tax and National Insurance in the normal way (if her earnings are over the minimum set by the Inland Revenue). Contact your local tax office if you are uncertain.

Additional Costs

In addition to her allowance, you should expect to pay automatically for her food and other basic living costs, such as heating and lighting, and for any expenses she incurs, for example if she takes the children swimming.

An au pair will need her own room, although she may have to

share a bathroom. She will often expect to have her own television. You will need to pay all her bills, although some families ask the au pair to contribute to the phone bill if she makes a lot of calls.

We asked au pairs whether they felt they were being paid a fair allowance, compared to other au pairs they knew, and 90 per cent of them said they felt they were; only 10 per cent said that they were not. Of host families, 55 per cent felt they were paying average rates, and 45 per cent felt they were paying more than the average.

Most people pay their au pair in cash.

OTHER BENEFITS

Bonuses

Bonuses can be given as a way of saying thank you and of rewarding your au pair, without having to increase your weekly costs.

Some host families pay their au pair a cash bonus if they are pleased with her. For example, you might choose to give her an extra week's pocket money before Christmas or on her birthday. Some give their au pair a bonus at the end of her stay, to thank her for her effort.

Sick pay

There are no regulations about whether or not you should pay your au pair pocket money when she is sick. However, good practice suggests that you should. If the sickness is serious or lasts a long time, she will probably want to go home anyway.

Other options

Additional benefits which you might wish to consider providing (and which were mentioned in our survey) include:

- Use of a car.
- Free use of a mobile phone and/or e-mail.
- The size and number/type of rooms provided for her own use will be a significant benefit, as will the frequency and type of holidays she takes with the family.

- Paid trips home.
- Having her friends and family to stay when they come to visit her.
- The cost of her language lessons (it is common for host families to pay for part or all of the cost).
- Additional holiday time.

SUMMARY

- There are clear Home Office guidelines on how many hours a week an au pair can help in the home and how much time off she must have.
- Some host families have 'au pair plus' arrangements with young people from EU countries, which allow them a little more help (at a higher cost).
- There are no guidelines on holiday entitlement, but it is good practice to give your au pair one week off for every six months she is with you.
- There are clear guidelines on how much pocket money an au pair should be paid as a minimum. In addition, you should take local rates into account.
- There are no guidelines on bonuses, or whether you pay your au pair when she is sick. However, it is good practice to be as generous as you can.
- Host families vary regarding the other benefits they provide their au pairs with. There are many options open to you. Good benefits may help you to keep your au pair for longer.

Part III:

Managing problems, boundaries and specific situations

10 Handling Issues, Crises and Gross Misconduct

'She ran up an enormous phone bill.' – Mum

'She left the children running around in a car park while she put the baby in the car.' – Mum

'I had a job where the mum overruled me on discipline in front of the children – it made it very hard for me.' – Nanny

All relationships are subject to ups and downs. In many circumstances, your relationship with your nanny or au pair can survive, and sometimes even grow, through issues and crises, if they are handled well.

WHAT ARE ISSUES, CRISES AND ACTS OF GROSS MISCONDUCT?

Issues are the small frustrations that both you and your nanny or au pair will experience with each other, the job and the children from time to time. For example, you may think that your nanny or au pair is neglecting her nursery duties, or she may feel that you undermine her in front of the children.

Crises are more significant. They are situations that make you question whether you want to continue to keep your nanny or au pair, for example if she has a major car accident. She may also consider whether she wants to stay with you, for example if you move away from the area.

An act of gross misconduct is an incident which is so severe that it may warrant terminating your nanny's contract or au pair's visit, sometimes without notice, for example theft or child abuse.

It is important that you can assess how serious a situation is, because issues, crises and acts of gross misconduct each merit different courses of action.

HOW TO HANDLE ISSUES

Employer's and host family's perspective

There are bound to be some issues, however minor, that will arise in your relationship with your nanny or au pair. There are a number of steps you need to follow to resolve them.

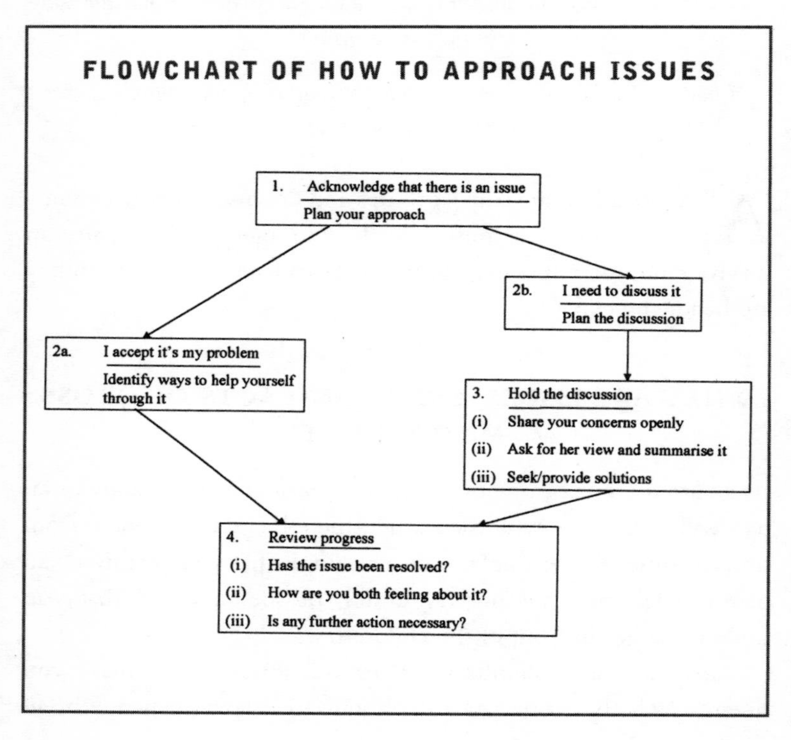

Step 1: Acknowledge that there is an issue

Reflect upon what bothers you and why. Be honest with yourself. Ask yourself who is responsible for the issue. Do you share the responsibility?

Plan how you will approach it. Do you need to say anything to your nanny or au pair? Is the issue solely your problem?

Step 2a: If you accept it's your problem

If you recognise that the issue is your problem, you need to identify ways to help yourself through it. For example, you could confide in a friend; you could rationalise it, for instance by making a list of pros and cons; or you could pamper yourself.

or

Step 2b: If you need to discuss it with her

If you are going to share the issue with your nanny or au pair, you will need to plan the content of your discussion. In particular, clarify what the issue is, why it bothers you, and what you would like to be done about it.

Step 3: Hold the discussion

In the discussion, be direct rather than apologetic. Say what the issue is and why it bothers you. Be honest. Try to stick to the facts, and avoid making personal remarks.

Invite your nanny or au pair to comment and give her perspective. Listen to her views and acknowledge them by summarising what she's said.

Then move forward. Ask her how you can both deal with it, or suggest what you would like done differently. Agree when you'll review progress.

Step 4: Review progress

Ask yourself, and your nanny or au pair, whether the issue has been resolved, how you both feel about it now, and whether any further action is necessary.

In our survey, employers and host families found that some issues come up quite often, and we offer some suggestions for dealing with them.

ISSUES FROM THE EMPLOYER'S AND HOST FAMILY'S PERSPECTIVE

Issue	Suggestions
Overtired at work	• Review her job responsibilities and ask yourself if you're asking too much of one person. • Ask live-in nannies/au pairs to reduce their mid-week socialising if this is an issue, and to be home at a reasonable time on Sunday evenings.
Indiscretion, gossiping	• Tell your nanny/au pair what you've heard and ask for her version. • Ask her not to disclose anything relating to your household to others and put this in her contract. • Don't encourage her to gossip about others, be careful what you tell her, and point out if it shouldn't be repeated.
Negligence (breakages, parking tickets, etc.)	• Accept that minor accidents will happen but expect to be told and to receive an apology. • Set a limit to the number that is acceptable (e.g. pay the first parking fine, but after that, ask her to reimburse you).
Prefers one child to another	• Point out what you've noticed and ask for her view. • Be clear that this is not acceptable and explain why. • Ask for and suggest ways of redressing the balance, e.g., activities to bond the less-favoured child and nanny/au pair.

Issue	Suggestions
Lacks experience/ common sense	• If you witness a specific situation, resolve the problem immediately. • Afterwards, sit down with your nanny/au pair and explain your concerns. • Suggest and agree a set of guidelines and safeguards, e.g., 'Before you put the baby down in the playroom, check the floor for small objects.' • Monitor progress.
Uses inappropriate language	• Allow for differences in dialect and upbringing. • Tell your nanny/au pair your preferred word and ask her to use that instead, e.g., 'Could you use "wet your pants" instead of "peed yourself"?' • Correct your child when he/she uses inappropriate language.
Spends excessive time on the phone during the day	• Tell her why long phone conversations aren't appropriate e.g. the children's needs are neglected. • Provide a guideline (e.g., two minutes) on length of calls. • Recommend that her friends ring her in the evening. • If people ring her at inconvenient times and you're there, ask them to call back after work.
Has daytime visitors to meet her needs rather than the children's	• Ask her to ensure that all social activities are child-focused. • Suggest that she meets her friends after work.

Issue	Suggestions
Excessive socialising during the day	• Provide a limit to the number of visits/visitors per week. • Ask for the children to spend some time by themselves each day for creative/quiet play.
Neglects nursery duties	• Point out what is being neglected and why it matters. • Review whether she has too much on and if the nursery duties are feasible. Ask her if all her duties are child-focused and whether she agrees with them. • Help her schedule her time, e.g., suggest that she does specific duties on certain days and leaves the other days free for more sociable activities.
Dislikes fresh air	• Find out why she prefers to stay indoors. • Discuss your children's physical needs with her. • Suggest exciting outings, e.g. to theme parks, and ways of managing them.
Doesn't mix well	• Ask her why she prefers to stay at home with the children. Talk to her about the children's social needs. • Provide a guideline on social activities, e.g. two outings to friends each week. • Invite the children's friends round to play.
Poor English (au pairs)	• Encourage her to attend her language classes.

Issue	Suggestions
	• Speak to her often and develop her skills. • Don't leave her in sole charge, until she can make herself understood.
Forgetful, e.g. late school pick-up	• Ask her what happened. There may be a good reason. • Ask her to reflect on the consequences for the children. • Ask her to apologise to the child and whoever else was inconvenienced. • Encourage her to think of ways of addressing the problem, e.g., leaving home earlier.
Lets the children do things you don't approve of, e.g., watch TV during the day	• Be clear about what is and isn't acceptable and how often your children can do certain activities, e.g., have ice creams, eat sweets, watch videos, visit McDonald's. • If you feel that this is being abused, ban the activity altogether during the week.
Loud music in the house after work; too many personal visitors (live-in nannies and au pairs)	• Ask her to reduce the noise when it's bothering you. • Provide guidelines, e.g. no music after 10.30 pm, or no more than five visitors at any one time. • Buy her some headphones.
Makes/receives excessive phone calls in the evenings (live-in nannies and au pairs)	• Limit the time and length of the calls, e.g., three calls between 7 and 10.30 pm of up to ten minutes' duration. • Fit a pay phone.

Issue	Suggestions
	• Get her her own phone line and ask her to pay the bill. • Put in an intercom to save you shouting up the stairs.
Is homesick/depressed (live-in nannies and au pairs)	• Discuss how she's feeling. Ask her what might help. • Invite her to participate in some family activities. • Allow her an extra phone call home a week/use of e-mail. • Contact the agency for a list of nannies/au pairs in the area, and invite some potential friends round.
Is late to work (mainly live-out nannies)	• Point out that she's often late and the impact that it has on the family. • Provide specific guidelines e.g. 'Could you be here for 7.55 am every day?'
Has excessive sickness (i.e., more than five separate occasions each year) (*In our survey 85% of nannies had less than one week off a year.*)	• Point out that her sickness level is unsatisfactory. • Discuss the impact of her sickness on the family. • Start the disciplinary warnings process if she makes no effort to improve her sickness record. • If she has a lot of time off sick, agree a limit to her sick pay.
Isn't flexible with reasonable requests	• Ask for her reasons for refusing to help.

Issue	Suggestions
	• If you think it's unreasonable and the tasks are part of her contract, point this out. You may have to start the disciplinary process. • If the task is outside her contract, she has a right to refuse. Offer to compensate her in some mutually acceptable way, e.g., time off in lieu, extra cash.
Dresses inappropriately for work	• This is a sensitive issue as it is a matter of personal taste. • Say why you think the clothes are unsuitable and give guidelines on what is more appropriate, e.g., something she has worn before that was suitable. • For live-in nannies and au pairs: she can wear what she wants when she's not working.
Has been with us for a while and is no longer making an effort	• Find out what her longer-term plans are and how long she wants to stay with you. • Give her feedback about her declining performance, providing specific examples. • Identify some new responsibilities and challenges for her if she is bored. Alternatively, suggest ways of developing her knowledge and skills in preparation for her next career move, e.g., through a local training course.

Issue	Suggestions
Moody behaviour	• Find out what lies behind it. • Point out the behaviour and explain its impact on the household. • Agree an alternative way of behaving and seek solutions to address the underlying issues.

Host family perspectives: Au pair issues

'I had an au pair with very bad acne. Unfortunately, she was self-conscious about the condition of her skin and was reluctant to socialise with other families and friends. She spent a lot of time in her bedroom. I was concerned about her. I felt she must be lonely and that it was unhealthy to spend so much time indoors during the summer. It wasn't much fun for the children either. I invited friends' au pairs round to the house and she became friends with one of them.'

****

'We had an au pair who could be moody and rude at times. We took her away with us when we went to stay with friends for the weekend and she sat in the corner scowling with her arms crossed. She never once said "please" and "thank you" and I was irritated and embarrassed by her behaviour. I talked to her about how she came across. She had no idea. She made a bit more effort after that.'

****

'Our au pair went out for dinner to a restaurant with a "blind date". We were concerned about the plan and advised her not to go. She insisted that it would be fine. At about 11.30 pm, we had a phone call from her. She was very upset. Her blind date had become frustrated when she had rejected his advances. He'd done a "runner" and left her at the restaurant with the bill. She didn't have enough money to pay it. We ended up having to drive into town, settle the bill and bring her home. She was more choosy about who she went out with after that.'

Issues from the nanny's or au pair's perspective

Your nanny or au pair may also experience problems related to your behaviour. They may occur when you are under pressure or when there is a temporary or permanent change in the situation at home, for example when you are on maternity leave.

Ideally she will raise the issue with you, but in reality many nannies and au pairs feel unable to put their views across. As the proprietor of a nanny agency explained, 'Nannies often feel that employers bark instructions at them and they find it difficult to respond successfully. Many of the training courses which nannies attend focus on nursery environments and do not include how to put your views across in an assertive manner to an employer.' Au pairs can find it difficult to express themselves well in another language.

If you want your relationship to be harmonious, you need to look out for signs of tension, both verbal and non-verbal.

SIGNS OF TENSION

Verbal signs	Non-verbal signs
More irritable with the children	Unusually keen to get away from the job at the end of the day
Increased level of complaints	Avoids eye contact with you
Flatter tone when describing the day	Smiles less; is more sullen
Less talkative than normal	Looks pale and tired
Sarcastic	Increased level of sickness or lateness

There are three steps you can take to resolve the problem. Firstly, acknowledge the change in behaviour or the issue. Then discuss it, and finally review progress.

Step one: Acknowledge the change in behaviour
Point out the change in behaviour. For example, 'you seem quieter than normal. How are things going?' Ask open questions rather than closed ones. If you ask a closed question like 'Is anything wrong?' It is easier for her merely to say, 'No,' and more difficult for you to ask further questions.

Step two: Discuss the issue
Having acknowledged that there is an issue, you need to address it. Let your nanny or au pair talk and repeat some of the words she uses. When she has given her view, summarise it to check that you've understood. Empathise with her, or put your own view across, if it is different. Ask what would help. If she doesn't know, make some suggestions. Agree a course of action and when you're going to review progress.

Step three: Review progress
Ask your nanny or au pair if the issue has been resolved, how she feels about it now, and whether any further action is necessary.

EXAMPLE OF A DISCUSSION ABOUT WHAT IS BOTHERING YOUR NANNY OR AU PAIR

Employer: 'You seem quieter than normal. How are things going?'

Nanny: 'Fine. Well, I'm a bit tired but everything's fine.'

Employer: 'A bit tired?'

Nanny: 'Yes. I'm having trouble sleeping at night, even though I'm exhausted. One of the boys is being quite a handful at the moment. I think the children are tired as it's the end of term and they are excited about the holidays. We're all tired.'

Employer: 'So the children are harder work at the moment and you're feeling exhausted.'

Nanny: 'Yes, but we'll get through it. I'm really looking forward to the break over Christmas.'

Employer: 'Good, but that's three weeks away. What would help you in the meantime?'

Nanny: 'Well, I'm finding it hard to manage all the after-school activities. Monday and Tuesday evenings are so hectic.'

Employer: 'Which is the most difficult?'

Nanny: 'Swimming on a Monday. It's a real rush to get them there, changed and in the pool by 4.30 pm.'

Employer: 'Why don't I find out if they do any weekend classes? If not, we could always drop the activity, as the boys will be swimming with the school soon. How would that affect things?'

Nanny: 'It'd make life a lot easier. Monday is such a heavy day at the moment. I feel exhausted for the rest of the week.'

Employer: 'Is there anything else that would help?'

Nanny: 'Perhaps if you ask the older boys to help me a bit more with the younger ones.'

Employer: 'I'll do that. Perhaps we could reward them for their efforts with football stickers, one sticker for each helpful day.'

Nanny: 'I'm sure that'll work a treat.'

Employer: 'So I'll phone up the pool and ask about alternative classes and get some football stickers in. Anything else?'

Nanny: 'No that would help a lot. I feel better for having told you.'

Employer: 'Good. Well, I'll come back to you later on about the classes, and let's review things in a week's time.'

Nanny: 'Thanks.'

The next table lists typical issues from nannies' and au pairs' perspectives, and suggestions for dealing with them.

ISSUES FROM THE NANNY'S AND AU PAIR'S PERSPECTIVE AND SUGGESTIONS FOR DEALING WITH THEM

Issue	Suggestions
It's not sole charge (nannies only) *(In our survey, 27% of nannies did not have sole charge all of the time)*	• Reflect upon why you aren't giving her a free rein. Be honest with yourself. • Identify ways of increasing her responsibilities which you both feel comfortable with.
Parents at home	• Children tend to act differently when their parents are around. Acknowledge this and establish some ground rules. • When your child asks you for something, involve your nanny/au pair in the decision, and support the position she takes. If you disagree, discuss it in private with her. • Try to help at critical times, e.g., participate in the school runs, make lunch, take a visiting friend home.
Lack of cash for outings *(In our survey, 10% of nannies felt that they weren't given enough cash to organise the children's activities)*	• Calculate what you can afford each week. Try to be more generous during the school holidays. • Explain your budget to your nanny/au pair and any procedure you want her to follow, e.g., keeping receipts. • Buy her a guidebook on activities for children and point out what can be done for free.

Issue	Suggestions
Lateness of parent	• Listen to your nanny's/au pair's views and consider how it affects her. • Provide notice whenever possible. • Pay overtime at a good rate. • If you can't keep to the hours in the contract, try to renegotiate her contracted hours and increase her pay accordingly. • When you are late and haven't given her any warning, reward her for her flexibility with extra cash or a small treat, e.g., cinema vouchers.
Critical parent undermining the nanny's/au pair's confidence	• You need to build up your nanny's/au pair's confidence. • Make a list of all the things she does well and praise her for them. • Reward your nanny/au pair for particularly hard work; e.g., give her a small present for organising your child's birthday.
Discipline is undermined by parent *(10% of nannies in our survey, didn't feel supported by the parents when disciplining the children)*	• Don't contradict your nanny's/au pair's decision in front of the children, unless the decision threatens their safety. • Discuss the issue later so that you can understand her viewpoint and put across your views too. Let small matters go.
Lack of communication with parent	• There may be important information about the children that you are missing out on. • Poor communication is de-motivating for your nanny/au pair. It reduces the value of what she does.

Issue	Suggestions
	• Allow at least ten minutes a day for a handover period. • Every month, put aside time without the children, to have a more lengthy review about how things are going.
Different values, ways of behaving, e.g., language, nudity, religious beliefs, boyfriends staying overnight	• Discuss the difference in your backgrounds and values. Try to understand your nanny's/au pair's perspective and respect her view, even if it's different from your own. • Agree a compromise, e.g., 'You can have a steady boyfriend to stay, once we've met him.' • If you're not prepared to compromise, accept that you may lose your nanny/au pair.
No privacy (live-in nannies/au pairs)	• Help your nanny/au pair to have as much privacy as possible by asking your children to stay out of her room unless invited in by her, and, of course, don't snoop yourself. Agree bathroom times if she shares a bathroom. • Think about ways of making her more self-sufficient, e.g. by providing a small fridge, kettle, TV and telephone in her room.
Can't entertain and/or have people to stay after work (live-in nannies/au pairs)	• Ask your nanny/au pair how this affects her. She may be lonely or it may put a strain on her relationships. • Discuss her needs and see if you can compromise. • Be aware that you could lose her if you ignore her social needs.

Issue	Suggestions
Poor pay *(In our survey, 15% of nannies and 10% of au pairs felt underpaid)*	• Listen to your nanny's/au pair's view and reflect upon it. • Contact local agencies and ask what the going rate is. • If you feel that she has a point, increase her pay to market rates. • If you can't afford to do so, be honest about it. Admit that she's underpaid and try to provide other benefits, such as additional holiday.

HOW TO RECOGNISE AND DEAL WITH CRISES

Crises are serious situations which make you, or your nanny or au pair, review whether or not you wish to continue your relationship. There are many different reasons why crises occur. Most of them fall into one of three categories, and each category needs to be approached differently.

EXAMPLES OF MAJOR CRISES

Changes in circumstances	Nanny or au pair's poor performance or misconduct	Employer's, host family's or children's behaviour
Nanny/au pair or parent becomes pregnant	Criticising the family to others	Employer/host family stops paying salary/pocket money
Long-term illness on part of nanny/au pair or parent	Major car accident, or driving ban	Children are persistently rude and/or violent
	Lying, deceit	
	Flirting with parent	

Changes in circumstances	Nanny or au pair's poor performance or misconduct	Employer's, host family's or children's behaviour
Nanny/au pair is contemplating a life change, e.g., getting married or embarking on a new career	Excessive sickness	Deteriorating living conditions
Parent is made redundant, or stops work	Persistent lateness	Inappropriate behaviour, e.g., parent flirting with nanny/au pair
Family moves out of area	Incompetent performance	Employer insists on unreasonable hours, activities, etc.
Children are all at school now	Major personality clash	
Parents separate/divorce		
Extreme loneliness, depression		

Changes in circumstances

Step one: Allow time for reflection

The first step when handling a change in circumstances is to allow time for the news to sink in. If the issue is new to your nanny or au pair, tell her and allow her some thinking time too. Don't just react. Do some research. Ask an agency or friends for ideas. Reflect on the available options, and fix a time to discuss them with your nanny or au pair.

Step two: Discuss the options

Seek her views but be honest about your boundaries. For instance, you might say, 'I wouldn't feel comfortable if your fiancé moved in with us, but I'd be happy to employ you as a live-out nanny.'

Step three: Agree a course of action

Finally, agree a course of action. Try to be flexible, because the circumstances might change again. Be honest, and discuss your concerns. Be realistic, too. Sometimes you may have to change your nanny or au pair.

Here are a couple of more detailed examples of crises arising from changes in circumstances.

Employer perspective: Lucy became pregnant

'Lucy had worked as a live-out nanny for me for six years. She became pregnant and asked me if she could continue to work for me on a part-time basis and bring her baby to work. I thought about it. I agreed to give the arrangement a go because I wanted to keep employing Lucy. I worked part-time myself and only one of my children was at home during the day. On the whole, the arrangement worked well. There were some small niggles. Lucy became less flexible about baby-sitting and she often asked my son to do errands for her baby, which I resented. But overall I was happy. We kept our nanny and Lucy kept a job she enjoyed and could combine with motherhood.'

Host family perspective: Fateful trip

'I had a lovely au pair from Sweden who asked to go home for Easter after she'd been with us for two months. Her grandmother was ill and she missed her boyfriend, who was doing his military service. Soon after she returned from her holiday, she told me that she thought that she might be pregnant. She was distraught about it and didn't know what to do. I tried to help her but she didn't want my help. She was also worried about her grandmother's health. In the end, she decided to return home, which was a shame for us, but probably the right decision in the circumstances.'

Employer perspective: An alternative career

'Suzanne had worked for us as a live-in nanny for two years. Unfortunately, my partner, Bob, lost his job following a merger at work. We reviewed our life plans. I was happy working in the City, but Bob saw his redundancy as an opportunity to change direction and to pursue his hobby, writing. Our youngest daughter was now at nursery every morning and in six months' time would be starting full-time school. As soon as Bob's redundancy happened, we both told Suzanne about it and said that we needed time to reflect. Two weeks later, we had supper together and Bob told Suzanne about his plan to write. We identified a number of options. She could stay with us for six months and then find an alternative job; however, Bob would be around at home. Suzanne could leave and Bob would look after our daughter in the afternoons until September, or Suzanne could stay on as our nanny but after September, we would need to find a nanny share to occupy her during the day and contribute to the cost.

Suzanne reflected upon the options and her own needs. She decided that she'd like to stay until September, and in the meantime buy and decorate her own flat. From September onwards she'd work as a full-time live-out nanny for another family. We were happy with the arrangement, as it gave us time to get used to losing Suzanne, and it would save us money in the longer term. Suzanne was upset at the thought of leaving, but felt that it gave her the opportunity to become more independent and time to prepare for the change.'

Nanny's or au pair's poor performance or misconduct

Poor performance or misconduct can merit disciplinary action being taken. In this case, there are some basic principles which should govern the way in which you handle disciplinary problems.

- Individuals should know their responsibilities, the standards of performance they are expected to achieve, and the house rules to which they are expected to conform.
- They should be given a clear indication of where they are failing or have broken the rules.
- Except in cases of gross misconduct, they should be given an opportunity to improve before disciplinary action is taken.

Taking disciplinary action

Dealing with disciplinary problems at home is similar to doing so at work. Except in cases of gross misconduct, you should follow a three-stage procedure:

1. An informal verbal warning
2. A formal verbal warning, which in serious cases may also be made in writing (these warnings should set out the nature of the problem and the likely consequences of further recurrences)
3. A final warning, in writing, which should contain a statement that any recurrence will lead to suspension, dismissal or some other penalty.

In practice, sometimes the disciplinary process is cut short because of the emotional nature of the relationship. One party becomes fed up with the situation, gives notice and ends the relationship.

The disciplinary process does not apply to au pairs, because they are not employees. However, if you are concerned about how your au pair is carrying out the activities you have asked her to do, or if you have concerns about her general conduct, it is appropriate and fair to follow a similar process: talk to her about it, and give her several chances to rectify the situation before asking her to leave. We have therefore referred to au pairs as well as nannies in the text.

The steps for dealing with each stage of a disciplinary situation are given below.

Step 1: Take time to reflect on the situation

How serious is it? Is it gross misconduct, in which case you may wish to dismiss your nanny or ask your au pair to leave? Cases of poor performance or misconduct merit a discussion, sometimes with a warning being given to the nanny and time allowed for her to improve.

Step 2: Ask for a meeting

Let your nanny or au pair know the nature and severity of the situation. Arrange a time to discuss the matter, when the children are not around. As a guideline, your discussion should occur within twenty-four hours of the incident. In the meantime, consult others, including your agency (if appropriate), for advice.

Step 3: Give your nanny or au pair the opportunity to state her case before deciding what to do

In particular, listen to her views and summarise them. Express your views and feelings. Try to stick to the facts and avoid making personal remarks.

State what action – e.g., a final written warning – you are going to take. Spell out the problem and the likely consequences of further recurrences of the same nature e.g. 'if you crash the car again, we will have to dismiss you'.

Step 4: Make a note of the warning (if relevant)

If you have given your nanny or au pair a warning, make a note of the warning and give your nanny or au pair a copy. If you found her via an agency, let them know what has happened.

Step 5: Agree a review period

Discuss and agree when you'll review matters to assess whether the situation has improved.

If this procedure is followed, an issue or crisis can often be resolved without your having to dismiss your nanny or au pair, as the following examples show.

Employer perspective: Poor driving skills

'Liz, our live-out nanny, had a car accident at work. She was parking our automatic car and put it into reverse by mistake.

As a consequence, the car required a new rear door and there was £500 worth of damage to the neighbour's car. Luckily no one was injured. All of this was covered by the insurance policy, but the premium increased substantially as a result. We gave Liz an informal warning and provided her with a smaller car to drive. Two months later she had another accident. This time she went into the back of a car in traffic. There was only a slight dent to our car but the other car was quite damaged. Again, the insurers paid but increased the premium. We had now lost both our no-claims bonuses. Liz was a good nanny in all other respects, but we were very worried about her driving skills. We sat down with Liz and gave her a formal warning, which we put into writing. We pointed out that, if Liz had any more crashes within a six-month period, she would have to go. We also said that in all other respects we were pleased with her performance. Liz was upset but felt that the warning was justified. She had been afraid that she'd lose her job. Over the next six months she drove carefully and avoided any further accidents.'

Employer perspective: Excessive time off work

'Wendy worked as our live-out nanny. She was an excellent nanny in many ways, but she persistently took time off for various reasons. Over a six-month period she had fifteen days off in total, on five separate occasions. These reasons included looking after a sick relative, flu, migraines and a burst pipe. I believed all the reasons to be genuine and empathised with Wendy over her bad luck, but I found it difficult to maintain my credibility as a director of a business when I had to cancel appointments because of Wendy's time off work. After the first five periods of time off, I reluctantly gave Wendy an informal oral warning. Wendy said that she understood, but then had a further absence. Wendy took three days off work after being mugged. She was not hurt, but had been frightened by the experience. I felt mean but I gave her a formal oral warning which I put into writing and said that any more absences over the next three months would result in a final written warning whatever the reason. Wendy only had one further day off sick that year.'

The employer's, host family's or children's behaviour

Sometimes nannies and au pairs reach the point where they are not sure they can continue to work for you, because of some aspect of their relationship with you or the children.

Again, there are four key steps in resolving such situations.

Step 1: Take the issue seriously

If your nanny or au pair raises a problem with you, listen to her concerns and avoid being defensive. Ask clarifying questions and seek some specific examples if it helps. Summarise her point of view, and then respond. You can ask for time to reflect on it, if you feel that would help.

Step 2: Provide a response

Respond with your perspective on the situation. Keep your discussion to the facts and don't make personal remarks, even if she did. If you really want to keep your nanny or au pair, you must be reasonable.

Step 3: Identify and agree a course of action

Ask your nanny or au pair for suggestions and agree a course of action. Agree when you'll review how it's going.

Step 4: Review progress

Discuss how you both feel about the situation now, whether actions taken have improved matters, and whether any more needs to be done.

HOW TO DISMISS YOUR NANNY OR ASK YOUR AU PAIR TO LEAVE

When gross misconduct has occurred you have the right to dismiss your nanny. Your contract of employment should stipulate what gross misconduct is and in what circumstances you can dismiss her without notice.

Au pairs are guests, not employees, and therefore cannot be dismissed and do not have the right to claim unfair dismissal. They can be asked to leave, if necessary. Obviously, you could ask your au pair to leave without giving a reason, but it is good practice to follow steps similar to those you would take for a nanny. We have therefore included au pairs in the text.

Some examples of gross misconduct are:

- Theft
- Drunkenness
- Illegal drug-taking
- Child abuse
- Threatening behaviour
- Endangering the safety of a member or friend of the family

Step 1: Ensure that you have good reason to dismiss your nanny or to ask your au pair to leave

For nannies, you need to check whether the offence is specified in your written contract of employment as one which might give rise to disciplinary action or to summary dismissal. If in doubt, seek advice from an agency, an employment lawyer or the Professional Association of Nursery Nurses (PANN).

Step 2: Hold a disciplinary meeting and explain the appeals process

Arrange to talk to your nanny or au pair away from the children. State what the offence is, and point out that you consider it to be gross misconduct. With a nanny, refer to her contract of employment and explain how she has broken it by her action.

Seek her views, and summarise them. Give your response. If you would like time to reconsider your position, say so. If you are convinced that you wish to dismiss her, tell her so. Specify what notice, if any, she has.

If you are dismissing her without notice, allow her time to gather her things and to say goodbye. A live-out nanny could leave relatively quickly, say within one hour. A live-in nanny or au pair will require longer to arrange alternative accommodation. You will need to give her at least twenty-four hours to move out, and an au pair might need some additional support.

For a nanny, make sure you write to her, explaining the reasons for her dismissal and giving her the opportunity to appeal (you should already have agreed a mutually acceptable person to whom the nanny can appeal in the event of dismissal).

Step 3: End the relationship in a civil manner

Following her dismissal there are a number of things you will need to do.

Think about what you will say to the children, and break the news to them yourself. Try to end the relationship and say goodbye in a civil manner. She may stay in the area, and it can be embarrassing for you and your children if you don't end the relationship properly.

If appropriate, let the agency know what has happened, so that they are in no doubt about her behaviour. An au pair agency may be able to help find a departing au pair temporary accommodation. In addition, the agency can start to search for a replacement for you and arrange temporary cover, if necessary.

Calculate what you owe her in wages, including pay for any outstanding holidays. Deduct any bills that you agreed in advance that she would pay, such as the telephone. Let the tax office know that she has ceased her employment with you.

Unfair dismissal (nannies only)

The law of unfair dismissal in the UK applies to employees with more than one year's service. When assessing whether or not a dismissal is fair, a tribunal asks itself the following questions.

1 Has the employee been there for more than one year?
2 Was the manner of the dismissal correct? That is, did the employer follow a proper procedure, giving fair warning of the consequences of continued misconduct or incapability?
3 Was the employer's decision to dismiss based on sufficient evidence?
4 Did the employee's offence or misbehaviour merit the penalty of dismissal, or would a lesser penalty have been appropriate in the circumstances?
5 Were there any mitigating circumstances which the employer should have taken into account?
6 Is there a proper and agreed appeals process in place, and was it followed?

Nannies from overseas who have valid work permits have the same right as UK nannies to claim for unfair dismissal after one year's service. In addition, employees with less than a year's service can claim unfair dismissal under certain circumstances, for example, if a nanny is dismissed because she is pregnant. Obviously, nannies with less than a year's service are entitled to proper notice. Contact your agency or an employment lawyer or PANN to check your employee's rights.

Employer perspective: Theft

'I had employed Angela as a live-in nanny for a year. She looked after my daughter, Lauren, who was three years old. I worked full-time and believed that my child had a varied social life, consisting of classes and outings. During the Christmas holidays, I decided to give the kitchen a good clear-out. I included Angela's drawer in the process. In the drawer I found Angela's diary. I know that I shouldn't have done this, but I started to read the entries and to my surprise found that on most days Lauren was taken to Angela's mother's and often left there. I rang up the various clubs that I had subscribed to for Lauren and found that she wasn't registered. I felt guilty about having read the diary but very angry about the deception. I'd spent several hundred pounds on club fees and, as the money was missing, I considered it to be theft. When Angela returned to work, I confronted her about the deception and Angela admitted that she had taken Lauren to her mother's and spent the club fees. I decided to dismiss Angela. Angela's contract had stated that theft was gross misconduct, and would result in dismissal without notice. Angela asked me to reconsider but I felt that I could no longer trust Angela and that the relationship had broken down irretrievably.'

Host family perspective: Child abuse

'We had an au pair called Paola to help look after our two sons, Stephen and Philip. It was her first time in the UK, and she'd been with the family for about two months. The boys did not seem to be particularly fond of her, but I thought this was because they'd been very attached to the previous au pair. One evening I received a call from my friend Helen. Helen told me that her nanny, Beth, had seen Paola shout at and hit Stephen, when he had wet himself. Beth felt that Stephen was scared of Paola; he seemed to recoil when she went near him. We were very upset to hear this. I had quite clearly said to Paola that she was not to hit either child. We decided to speak to Paola about it. Paola became very angry. She burst into tears and denied having shouted at or hit Stephen. We felt in a difficult position. We reiterated that she was not to hit the children and that we would like her to be supportive when Stephen wet himself. Two weeks later I was talking to a neighbour. The neighbour said that she felt she ought to let me know that she'd seen Paola smack Philip when he threw his plate on the floor, while they were having tea in the garden. We decided that we felt uncomfortable leaving our boys with Paola. Despite the warning, Paola had continued to hit the children. I spoke to the agency, who agreed that

Paola's behaviour was not acceptable. We then spoke to Paola about it. Paola denied having hit Philip. She said that there was a conspiracy against her. Again, she became very angry and she called me a liar. We asked Paola to leave because she had hit the children and we couldn't trust her any more. We considered that this was tantamount to child abuse. We gave Paola a week to find alternative accommodation, but didn't leave the children in her care again. She left two days later, saying she was returning home because she was homesick.'

NANNY-SHARE ISSUES AND CRISES

Nanny-share arrangements suffer from their own distinct set of issues and crises related to the relationship between the two families. The following are among the more common.

- One set of parents becomes less flexible (e.g., wants the arrangement at their home all of the time).
- Circumstances change (e.g., expecting another child, moving area).
- Pay issues, such as arguments over the proportions of salary paid, or of expenses provided.
- Different values and requirements (e.g., one set of parents is less happy about the nanny's performance).
- Petty disputes, such as niggles about holidays, food provided, etc.
- The nanny prefers one family or child to the other.

It is quite common for the relationship between families involved in a nanny share to deteriorate over time. Our tips for ensuring a good nanny-share relationship are:

- Socialise together, and regularly review (e.g., monthly) how it's going.
- Be honest and open with each other about issues, however small. Don't let things escalate.

- Avoid gossiping about the other family to the nanny, and don't allow her to play one family off against the other.
- If an issue needs raising with your nanny, discuss it with the other parents first, and agree how to approach it and what actions you both wish to take.
- When dealing with issues, crises and performance reviews, see your nanny together, so as to present a united front.
- If it's not working, say so, and end the arrangement before things turn sour.

Employer perspective: Breakdown of the nanny-share arrangement

'I met Sarah through post-natal exercise classes, and we decided to share a nanny. We got on well and were both returning to work at the same time. We went out for dinner with our husbands and agreed what sort of cover we needed, what we were prepared to pay and how the nanny share would be organised. The two of us then recruited a nanny together. We employed Virginia, whom we both liked. Everything was fine for the first three months. Then I noticed that Virginia seemed rather low and pale. When I asked her what was wrong, Virginia said that Sarah criticised the way she looked after the babies when the share was at her house. She felt undermined. I talked to Sarah about it. Sarah said that she wasn't sure that Virginia was up to the job. She said that she lacked initiative, was very slow and disorganised. I looked out for this when Virginia was at my house. I could see that Sarah had a point but thought that, on the whole, Virginia was a good nanny and very well suited to looking after babies. The babies seemed very happy in her care. Over the months the situation got worse. Sarah continued to undermine Virginia, despite my request to discuss any performance issues with me first. After eleven months, Sarah announced that she and Mark were moving away. I was secretly delighted. The nanny-share relationship had run its course and I wanted to employ Virginia by myself.'

SUMMARY

- All relationships are subject to ups and downs; handle each issue or crisis appropriately.
- Don't let issues get out of hand. Deal with them immediately.
- Recognise when your nanny or au pair is frustrated, and ask her why. Be prepared to adjust your behaviour.
- When dealing with a crisis, consider whether it has arisen because of a change in circumstances, because of the nanny's or au pair's performance or misconduct, or because of your own or the children's behaviour. Each needs to be dealt with differently.
- Respect your nanny's right to have sufficient warnings about any performance problems, and give her time to improve. Treat your au pair in the same way.
- If you have to dismiss your nanny or ask your au pair to leave, try to end the relationship in a civil manner.
- If you have a nanny-share arrangement, work at maintaining a good relationship with the other family in the share. Discuss all issues as they arise and agree how you will handle any issues, crises and performance reviews.

11 Managing the Boundaries

'Remember it's her job, not her life.' – Dad

'It's hard at the moment because the mum is at home on maternity leave and always meddling.' – Nanny

'Sometimes I don't know if I'm supposed to be part of the family, a guest or a worker.' – Au pair

The employer–nanny relationship is more emotional and intense than many other relationships because you are paying someone to look after your beloved children. In addition, the arrangement takes place in your own home and, naturally, you want things to be harmonious there; and it is more difficult to be objective about issues that are close to home.

This chapter focuses on how to establish boundaries with your nanny, and how to manage the boundaries when you are both around and when you are absent. The boundaries are slightly different for au pairs, as they are supposed to live with you as a member of your family, but some points are also relevant to au pairs, and where this is the case we have said so.

ESTABLISHING BOUNDARIES

It is important to establish clear boundaries with your nanny from the outset. She is an employee, not an intimate friend. Most people find it easier to manage someone if they do not get too close. You need to think about what information you are prepared to share with your nanny, and what you wish to keep private. You may find the following tips helpful.

- Explain to her why you have a nanny and what your personal needs and values are, so that she can understand you better.
- Don't disclose information about your personal relationships. For example, if you have an argument with your partner, don't tell your nanny the details.
- Clarify what you'd rather not know about your nanny (e.g., about her sex life), and don't seek or encourage information in this area.
- Avoid gossiping about others to her. If your nanny passes on some gossip to you, say that you'd rather not hear about another family's personal issues.
- When you do confide in her, clearly state what shouldn't be passed on to others and why.
- Invite your nanny (as a guest) to family events relating to the children, such as birthday parties and christenings, which take place outside her normal working hours, so that she feels part of the family.

Once you have established clear boundaries, you can develop a good, trusting relationship with your nanny.

You need to establish boundaries with an au pair too. As she is a guest, rather than an employee, you are likely to spend more time with her than you would with a live-in nanny. This will affect the nature of your relationship. However, the same principle applies: you need to think about how much you wish to share with your au pair and what, if anything, you wish to keep private. It may also be useful to think about how you can engineer time apart from each other.

At times you may find that you and your nanny have crossed the boundaries and become too close. This often happens when you have spent a lot of time together, on holiday, for example, or during maternity leave or sick leave. If this occurs, you need to review the situation and ask yourself, 'Am I comfortable with the closeness of our relationship?' and 'Can I still give my nanny honest feedback?'

If the answer to either question is 'No', you will have to try and re-establish your boundaries. You can do this by identifying how you became too close and avoiding the circumstances in which it happened, by spending less time together, and by discouraging heart-to-heart sessions on issues outside the children and job. An example follows.

Employer perspective: Portuguese disclosures

'Alice came on holiday with us to Portugal. Most evenings, we all had supper together. My husband, Nick, was exhausted and tended to go to bed after supper. Alice and I washed up and then shared a bottle of wine together. I enjoyed having someone to talk to. We talked into the night about our childhoods, hopes and fears.

'When we returned to England, I realised that Alice and I knew each other a lot better and that we were much closer as a result. However, I felt that I'd compromised my position as an employer. When I returned to work, I distanced myself from Alice a bit. When she was at home, we talked about the children but not about ourselves. I felt concerned that Alice might miss our intimate chats, but she didn't seem bothered by it. She was busy seeing her other friends in Yorkshire. I understood what made Alice tick a lot better, but decided not to refer to information gleaned over the Portuguese holiday again.'

MANAGING JEALOUSY

It is normal to envy your nanny at times. On a lovely sunny day, who wouldn't want to wear casual clothes and go for a picnic in the park, rather than put on a suit and travel to work? If you don't work, there may be times when you want to be alone with the children, instead of having someone else to consider and accommodate. However grateful you are that you have help, sometimes you may wish that you hadn't. In this section, we list possible situations involving jealousy, and suggest steps to take to handle them. Some of the situations may also apply to au pairs.

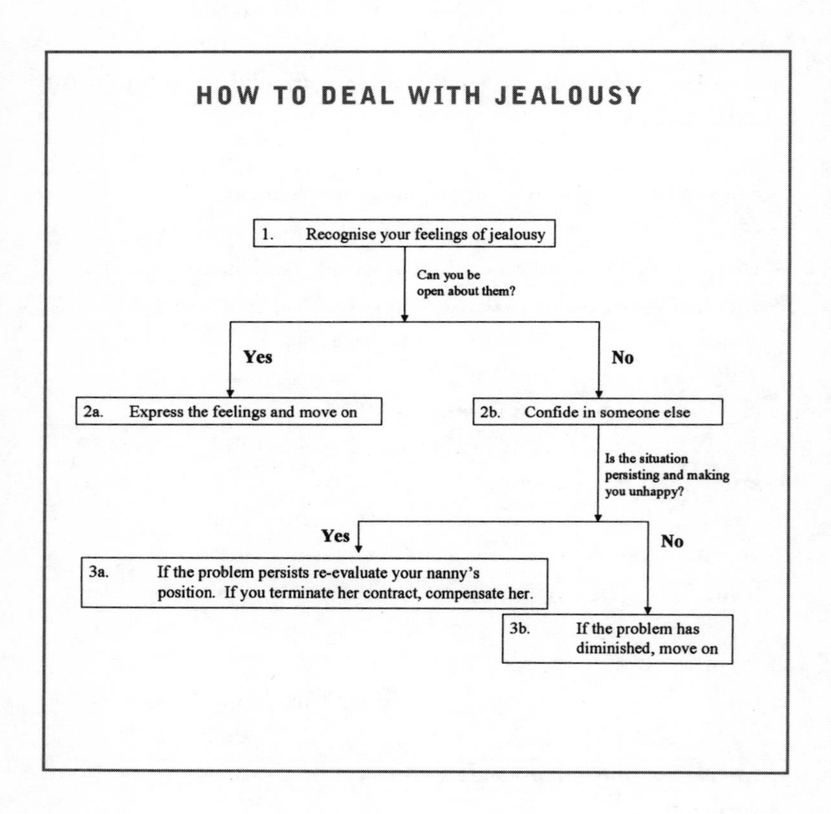

Step 1: Recognise your feelings of jealousy

Reflect upon what is making you jealous of your nanny and what impact it's having on your behaviour.

Step 2a: Express the feelings and move on

Be open about your jealousy when you feel that it will not hurt anyone or harm your relationship. For example, you could say, 'I really envy you going on your outing to the park. I'd much rather do that than get on a stuffy tube and go to work.' Once you've shared the feeling, it is less likely to leak out indirectly through sarcasm or sullen behaviour.

or

Step 2b: Confide in someone else

If your feelings cannot be shared with your nanny, because they might harm the relationship, try and confide in someone else about them. Consider if there is a real problem that needs to be addressed.

Step 3a: If the problem persists

Is the problem continuing to make you unhappy? If it is, you may need to re-evaluate your nanny's position for your own peace of mind. However, if you ask her to leave because of your jealousy, be honest about the reason, so that she understands why she has lost her job. When parents give a false reason – e.g., 'a personality clash' – it adds insult to injury and takes the nanny longer to get over the situation. If you terminate your nanny's contract because you envy her, you will need to compensate her, by paying her at least her notice period. In some circumstances, you may wish to pay her more for the inconvenience caused. With au pairs, you could try and find her another family to live with, or pay for her flight home.

or

Step 3b: If the problem diminishes

Has the problem diminished or gone away? If it has, you are very fortunate and can move on.

Employer perspective: A false start

'I wanted to return to work and found a nanny, Shirley, three months ahead through a local play group. Shirley and I met for coffee at regular intervals and we discussed my plans. We got on really well. However, when Shirley started the job she insisted that I kept out of the house so that the children could get used to me not being around. Towards the end of the second week, Shirley and I reviewed how the job was going.

It wasn't working out for me but I couldn't admit it. I felt excluded from my children and home. That evening, I couldn't stop crying. I realised that I didn't really want to have a nanny and return to work. I couldn't face Shirley – I knew that she'd be so disappointed. I asked Alan, my husband, to tell her. Alan gave Shirley two weeks' pay. This was made up of one week's pay for her notice, because she was still in her probationary period, plus an extra week's pay for the inconvenience of losing her job at short notice.'

Nanny perspective: The job that wasn't

'I applied for a job working in the Middle East for a member of a royal family there. Following an interview in London, I was offered the job and accepted it. I went out to the Middle East to start work. I was to have a week's handover with the departing nanny. I'd only been there for two days when I was told that the departing nanny had changed her mind and didn't want to leave. I was told that she felt jealous when she saw me with the children. She didn't want anyone else to look after them or to have her job. I was extremely disappointed, because I'd been looking forward to taking responsibility for the children and having the experience of working overseas. I was given twelve weeks' pay and sent home. However, in some ways it was a blessing. The job wasn't wholly as described at interview. For example, I had to sleep in the same room as the children, who were seven and nine, and I wasn't allowed to let them out of my sight. It was great to have the money and I bought an old VW Beetle to cheer myself up.'

SITUATIONS INVOLVING ENVY AND HOW TO DEAL WITH THEM

Your baby wants to return to your nanny when you pick him up.

Pros	Cons	Suggestions
• The nanny and baby have bonded well. • He is very secure in her care. • Your nanny may stay longer because of the bond.	• The baby may find it difficult when your nanny leaves. • She may prefer the baby to the other children and show favouritism. • It may be hurtful if the baby is less clingy with you.	• All babies go through a clingy stage from around 9 months. It is normal. • Ensure that your baby socialises with others during the day. • Watch out for favouritism if you have more than one child. • Spend special time with your baby when you can.

You miss a milestone in your child's development, e.g., his first steps.

Pros	Cons	Suggestions
• It is very motivating for your nanny to witness a milestone.	• You may feel that you're missing out on the exciting bits and you may question your focus in life.	• Try and share in your nanny's joy and don't reduce her pleasure at witnessing the event.

Pros	Cons	Suggestions
• If your nanny tells you, she is being honest. Some nannies hide these things from their employers so as not to upset them.		• He'll do it again soon, and the first time you see it will be the milestone for you.

You wish you were going on the children's outing, rather than going to work.

Pros	Cons	Suggestions
• Your maternal/paternal instincts are still intact. • Your children are having fun with your nanny.	• Work isn't exciting enough for you at the moment.	• Organise a similar treat for yourself at the weekend, or take a holiday. • There may be days when you're glad you're not at home; reflect on those times, too. • If you have these feelings a lot, you may need to reconsider how you spend your time.

The children ask for your nanny at weekends.

Pros	Cons	Suggestions
• Rejoice that they like her. It would be more worrying if they didn't mention her.	• You may be hurt by this.	• Tell her that they asked for her – she'll be flattered.

Pros	Cons	Suggestions
	• You may be treating the children differently in terms of discipline.	• Examine the circumstances in which it happened. Does she treat them differently, and should either of you alter your behaviour?

Your nanny needs reassurance from you about how fond the children are of her, and you find it hard to give.

Pros	Cons	Suggestions
• Your nanny cares how fond the children are of her.	• It can be difficult to express how fond the children are of someone else.	• Give her reassurance. It'll motivate her and she'll do a great job. • Don't worry about it. Just as you have enough love to share around, so do the children.

Your nanny or au pair has time to have fun – e.g., to go to parties or shopping – but you haven't.

Pros	Cons	Suggestions
• You have your own time too, but perhaps make different choices. • It's good that she has a life outside work and isn't lonely.	• Your nanny may be tired at work if she overdoes her weekend activities.	• If you feel her socialising is excessive, you could check for signs of tiredness. For example, is she short with the children after a late night out?

Pros	Cons	Suggestions
		• Try and show an interest in her and what she does. • Give yourself a treat while she's working.

You cannot go to sports day, and your daughter wins a race.

Pros	Cons	Suggestions
• It's good that someone was there to support your child.	• You wish you could have been there.	• Be grateful that someone was there to witness it and share her joy. • Ask the school for next year's date, and block the day off now in your diary.

Your nanny can relax at the weekend.

Pros	Cons	Suggestions
• She'll be refreshed for the week ahead.	• She may then have the energy to party all night and make you even more jealous!	• Organise a mid-week visit to a health club and pamper yourself for a change. • At the weekend, take it in turns to have a lie-in, if possible.

All your earnings go on paying for child care, and your nanny asks for an increase.

Pros	Cons	Suggestions
• You must enjoy your job if you're doing it for no gain. • You have another interest outside the children.	• You may resent paying over all your earnings, plus extras for outings, etc.	• Be honest about your financial situation, so that your nanny is aware of it and can be sensitive to it. • If you really can't afford an increase, say so, but perhaps think of other ways (e.g., extra holiday) to reward her.

Your nanny brings her baby to work. You miss your children during the day and resent the fact that she can work and be with her child too.

Pros	Cons	Suggestions
• Nannies with children are often more empathetic towards the parents. • She is likely to stay longer because it's a good arrangement for her.	• You may resent going to work to pay for child care while she doesn't need to. • You may resent your home being used as a crèche, especially if your children have grown out of that phase.	• Remember that you aren't having to do the boring bits during the week: she is. • If there aren't enough benefits for you in the arrangement, don't continue it.

Your nanny is thinner and fitter than you are.

Pros	Cons	Suggestions
• She'll be fitter for the job.	• She may remind you of how you used to look pre-children. • She may make you feel frumpy.	• Rejoice in having a fit, sleek nanny. It reflects well on you. • You could always buy her lots of sweets and cakes to graze on during the day!

You think your partner is attracted to your nanny.

Pros	Cons	Suggestions
• You have good taste – after all you chose both of them!	• You may feel uncomfortable about having temptation under your roof.	• Talk to him about your concerns. Find out if he really is attracted to her or just finds her aesthetically pleasing! • If you feel very uncomfortable about it, you may need to terminate her contract, but be honest about your reasons for doing so.

HOW TO MANAGE WHEN YOU'RE BOTH AROUND

Some nannies do not like the parents being around, because they find that the children behave differently and are more difficult to manage. If you will be around for some or all of the time, you need to make this clear during the interview, and ask the nanny how she feels about it. Even if you're normally absent, there may be times when you are at home (for example, if you are sick or on maternity leave).

Periods of time together work better once you have discussed who is responsible for what; how the job differs from the normal routine; ground rules for how you'll work together and any changes to contracted hours and pay.

Managing when you are both around is not such a big issue if you have an au pair. Au pairs do not expect to have sole charge of children under three years old, and, generally speaking, they spend less time supervising children by themselves. Nevertheless, many of the points – such as some of the issues and tips for going on holiday together – are applicable to au pairs too.

Working from home

Working from home can work well but it requires self-discipline on the part of the parents and patience on the part of the nanny. In our view, the nanny should have sole charge of the children, and you should avoid interfering, except in emergencies.

WORKING FROM HOME

Issues	Suggestions
The children come in and disturb you.	• Put a sign on the door saying when you can be disturbed and when you can't. • Close the door if you don't want to be interrupted. If that doesn't work you can always lock it!

Issues	Suggestions
You are disturbed when you are on the phone.	• Establish a signal for 'I'm not to be interrupted', so that the children know when to leave.
Your nanny keeps asking you to help out.	• Say 'No' when you need to, and don't feel guilty. She couldn't ask you if you worked elsewhere, and she shouldn't rely on your presence if she has sole charge.
The children want you.	• Spend some additional time with them. Organise your day so that when they come home from school, you spend time with them. After a while they'll be happy to go off and play.
	• Stay out of the way as much as possible. It is confusing if you appear and then disappear. The children will get upset and your nanny frustrated because she has to comfort them.
Your nanny sees you as a hindrance.	• Try and make a positive contribution during busy times, (e.g., do a school run, help out at bathtime) so that you are seen as an asset.
You hear something you don't agree with.	• Decide whether it really matters. If it doesn't, let it go. If it does, talk to your nanny about it later in private. Don't undermine her in front of the children.
Clients or colleagues are coming to the house and you need peace and quiet.	• Warn your nanny in advance and suggest she takes the children out during that time.

Issues	Suggestions
The children play the nanny and you off against each other.	• Defer to her during her working hours, ask the children to consult her. Back up her decisions, even if you'd have given a different response.
It's too noisy.	• Let your nanny know your schedule, so that she can arrange to be in when you're out and vice versa.

On maternity leave

When you take time off work or stop work altogether to have another baby, it is important that you envisage how your nanny and you will work together.

- Would you like your nanny to be involved in preparing for the arrival of the baby (e.g., cleaning clothes and equipment), or do you want to do it?
- What sort of cover arrangements will you require close to the baby's birth?
- Do you want sole charge of the baby during your maternity leave, or would you like your nanny to take the baby sometimes? If so, how often? Are you planning to do things with the other children?
- Are you expecting any help with the nights and, if so, are you prepared to pay extra?

Nannies will have their own views on how much they wish to be involved with the baby – some like to keep their normal routine going, others relish the thought of a baby and are very keen to spend some time with the new arrival. You will need to discuss how your nanny feels. You will also have to consider the extent to which her responsibilities are increasing, and pay her accordingly.

If your nanny is willing to be involved with the new baby from the start, there are benefits for you, your nanny and the other children. Your nanny gets to know the baby straight away, and your children get used to seeing them together and learn to accommodate the baby. The children can spend some time with you and don't have to compete with the baby. Moreover, you can get some rest when you're feeling exhausted.

Being on maternity leave and spending more time with your nanny presents some challenges. We have identified three common ones.

First, because you're around more, you see how your nanny does her job and you may become increasingly critical of her. Working alongside her, you notice and get irritated by small things, such as your nanny leaving bits at the bottom of the sink. It is better to let the small stuff go and focus on any major issues, so that you can keep things in perspective. Try to take a long view of the situation. If you like your nanny, it is worth keeping quiet so that she doesn't get de-motivated by your nit-picking. Make a list of what she's good at and what she does less well. If there are lots of positive aspects, focus on them. Then destroy your list. If you feel that the negatives outweigh the positive aspects, give her a performance review and look at ways she could address her weaker areas.

The second problem is that, when you're both around the home, you are bound to get under each other's feet a bit. Take the initiative and go out for a walk, visit a friend, etc. If you are housebound, be honest, say you'd like a rest, and ask her to give you some space. Develop a routine so that you use the kitchen at different times or have lunch in different rooms. There's an upside, too: it is sometimes nice to have company.

Lastly, your nanny may be insensitive to your feelings. Don't assume that she will understand how you feel before or following the birth of your baby. She may not have had a baby herself or, if she has, she may have had a very different experience. Tell her how you feel and ask for her help. Thank her for any sensitivity or flexibility shown.

Employer perspective: Close quarters

'I wasn't looking forward to being on maternity leave, because I thought that Jane, our daily nanny, would get on my nerves. Jane was a good nanny, but she talked all the time and had a tendency to repeat herself. I'm much more comfortable with silence.

'At first, after Joe was born, I was able to cope with Jane's talking. I even enjoyed having some company. But as my maternity leave went on, I found Jane's incessant talking irritating. I took steps to limit our time together, by spending time in my bedroom with the baby, and taking Joe for walks. I organised visits to friends to break up the week and went to visit my parents in Cornwall. At times I wanted to say something, but I felt that it was too personal and that Jane would be hurt. Jane was a friendly, outgoing person, and most of the time the children benefited from this. I never shared my frustration with Jane. One benefit was that in some ways, I looked forward to returning to my quiet office in town, at the end of my maternity leave!'

On sick leave

If you or your partner have to have time off work because you are ill, you may need peace and quiet to recover your strength. Be open with your nanny about your needs, and how your presence at home will affect her job. If you need looking after, consider getting in temporary additional help, as your nanny can't be expected to play nurse too. If she does offer to look after you, reward her for her extra efforts – and don't expect the service to continue once you've recovered!

Some issues that can arise when a parent is sick at home are:

- The house is very noisy. Be honest about your sleep requirements and ask your nanny to limit your children's visitors temporarily, or to go out so that you can rest.
- The children keep disturbing you. Put a note on the door when you're sleeping and reward them later for having stayed away.

- The nanny asks you to help when you need to rest. When you're exhausted, say 'no', you need to rest. Help out when you're feeling refreshed.
- The children want you. Spend some time each day doing quiet activities together. For example, read them stories, help with homework, or watch a video together, so that both the children and your nanny benefit from your being at home.

On holiday together

It is common for live-in nannies and au pairs to go on holiday with their employers. We have had really successful holidays with nannies over the years, but they haven't happened by accident and you need to plan and agree the arrangements in advance. You should be honest about what your expectations are, and what you will give your nanny in return.

Prior to the holiday

Ask your nanny or au pair if she would be willing to accompany you. If she says 'no', be grateful that she was honest. An unwilling nanny or au pair can ruin your holiday. If she says 'yes', you need to work out the following:

- What you'll pay her if additional hours are required (nannies only).
- What her hours will be.
- What accommodation she'll have. Ensure that she has her own room and some privacy. Advise her on what she'll need to take – including an alarm clock.
- Describe what the pattern of the days will be like. Discuss how you wish to share the child-minding duties and be clear about any responsibilities that will be solely hers, such as bathing the children at the end of the day. Ensure that you cover her duties on the journeys, too, as travel can be the most stressful part of a family holiday.
- Discuss how much time you wish to spend alone and provide facilities so that she can entertain the children. For example, some families take a second car on UK holidays, so that their nanny or au pair has more independence and can take the

children on outings. If there are few facilities available, limit the time you leave her alone to entertain the children, and take some books, art materials, toys and games with you.

- You might like to ask your nanny or au pair to pack for the children. We have devised a packing list (given in Appendix V) to make this easier to delegate.

During the holiday

When you are on holiday involve your nanny or au pair in some of the enjoyable parts of the holiday, such as meals out and outings. It will be a perk for her and also make the outings more relaxing for you.

If things are not working out as you envisaged, say so, and suggest alternative arrangements. Don't let her spoil your holiday. You could resent it for a long time.

At the end of the holiday discuss what aspects worked well and less well. If she has been flexible, you might like to buy her a present to recognise this.

Going on holiday with other families

Going on holiday with another family can be fraught if you do not discuss child care in advance, both with the other parents and with your nanny or au pair. In our experience, it works better when both families take a nanny or au pair so that one person does not end up looking after all the children. You will need to discuss with the other parents how much they are paying their nanny or how much pocket money they are giving their au pair; what hours they are expecting her to work; and what they expect her to do. The closer your views and treatment in these areas, the better the arrangement works.

If the other family is not taking a nanny or au pair, but would be happy to have some help, suggest to them that your nanny or au pair brings a friend along to provide the help. The benefits are that your nanny or au pair will have company and the other family will have an extra pair of hands to help with their children.

If you are the only ones with a nanny or au pair, you need to agree the boundaries of her job both with her and with the other parents. If she does end up helping the other family (e.g., by baby-sitting for them), suggest that they pay her for doing so, so as to minimise any resentment caused.

Taking nannies or au pairs on holiday does not always go to plan. The table below provides some potential issues and suggested courses of action.

HOLIDAYS

Issues	Suggestions
Your nanny/au pair oversleeps in the mornings.	• Be clear about what time you'd like her to start in the mornings. • Remind her that it's your holiday and a 'working holiday' for her (nannies only). • When you hear the children wake up, ask her to look after them if she's meant to be on duty. • If she's forgotten her alarm clock, buy her one.
The family you've gone on holiday with are abusing your nanny's/au pair's goodwill.	• Speak to her about it, and ask how much it is bothering her and what she would like to happen. Then speak to the other parents and ask them to stop or to reward your nanny/au pair, whichever she prefers. • Go on a couple of outings without the other family, giving her a break from the other children. • Give her some extra time off to recuperate and relax.
Your nanny/au pair is lonely.	• Do not leave her for whole days by herself with the children. If you want to go on outings, limit yourself to half a day at a time.

Issues	Suggestions
	• On her days off, offer to take her with you but don't expect her to work.
	• Allow and help her to phone home from time to time.
Your nanny isn't using her initiative as much as she does at home (nannies only).	• When you're on holiday, it is normal for her to defer to you more and to use her own initiative less.
	• Make suggestions about what she could do with the children, but leave the decision up to her.
	• Leave her in sole charge sometimes – she'll probably enjoy it.
You are travelling over the weekend and your nanny/au pair doesn't usually work then.	• Discuss working over the weekend with her in advance. Ask her if she would prefer another day off during the holiday or additional pay.
	• Ask for flexibility on hours. For example, if you don't arrive in the resort until late evening, ask her to work later, but be flexible yourself and give her a later start the next day.

Employer perspective: Tuscany

'We spent our summer holiday with our nanny, Tara, in Tuscany. It was quite an experience. A couple of days before departure, the travel agent phoned to say that they'd had to change the villa because the one we'd chosen was being repaired. The travel agent assured us that the new villa was of superior quality.

'The alternative villa was huge – it had several wings, a

sloping garden, a large lake and a guard dog tied to a tree. We had hoped to do some sightseeing without the children, but felt unable to leave Tara at the villa for long, because the villa and gardens were a 'death trap' for small children. Instead, we kept our absences to short trips and spent days on the beach together. Tara was a fabulous castle builder and was happy to help entertain the children. This meant that we could read our books occasionally. Tara proved to be pleasant company, not too dominating but game to join in.'

Nanny perspective: Going on holiday with your employer

'Going on holiday with a family is a big "no-no" for some nannies, as it can be a very difficult time. The main problem is having the parents around. The children are very different. They tend to play the nanny off against the parents, and they can really try to get away with things that they wouldn't normally be able to. Basically, when I've been on holiday with families, I have found that it is best to relax my regime and let the children get away with things. It's their holiday too.

'Good communication between the nanny and family is essential, so that problems faced on either side can be resolved. The holiday is enjoyable if there is some give and take, for example, if everyone mucks in and helps with cooking and playing with the children. When this happens, the holiday is more relaxing for everyone.'

Celebrating birthdays

Birthday parties are much easier when you have some help, and you may want to consider involving your nanny. If so, you'll need to find out how much experience she has of organising them, and to clarify which of the following tasks you want her to do or to help you with.

Before the party
- Draw up a guest list
- Decide the party theme
- Find a party entertainer (if relevant)
- Send out the invitations
- Keep track of responses and chase up late replies
- Prepare a shopping list and do the shopping
- Make or buy a cake
- Create the party bags
- Design the games
- Decorate the venue
- Prepare the food

During the party
- Welcome the guests
- Entertain the children and their parents
- Serve the food and the cake

After the party
- Clear up
- Give out the party bags
- Pay the party entertainer (if relevant)
- Open the presents
- Oversee the thank-you letters

Before the party, divide up the tasks with your nanny and discuss and agree the timescales. If the party is taking place over a weekend, discuss how your nanny will be remunerated. Close to the event, discuss the party timetable and responsibilities during and after the event. After the party, review how it went and provide a small gift in recognition of your nanny's additional efforts.

The first birthday party you organise together can involve some trial and error, and you will need to be clear about your needs. For example, if you find that your nanny spends a lot of time talking to the parents and you are running around like a headless chicken, ask her to do specific tasks – in these circumstances you'll need to be polite but firm. Talk to her about it afterwards, and be more specific about responsibilities before the next party.

If your child's birthday party is over the weekend, you may not be sure whether to invite your live-out nanny. It's a good idea to invite her, so that she feels part of the family. However, if she can't come don't be disappointed as she has her own life too. If she's coming as a guest, you don't need to pay her, but you shouldn't expect her to help, either. If you really need her help, ask her to do half a day over the weekend, and pay her for it.

Employer perspective: Halloween party

'One of our nannies, Alex, was very creative. Soon after she joined, I decided to have a Halloween party to integrate the children with their new school friends, and to give Alex a challenge to get her teeth into.

'We agreed on a guest list and discussed party food, but I left decorating the house and costumes to Alex, as she offered to do them and had some good ideas. I took care of the games.

'Alex created the most fabulous outfits for each child and made herself a spider costume. I was hoping to get away with jeans, but was strongly encouraged to go as a ghost. Alex decorated the basement of our house during the last hour before the party, turning it into a spooky den. I would never have made such an effort. The party taught me much about playing to a nanny's strengths and utilising her resources. The party was a great success and we all had a really enjoyable time.'

Joint outings

Many nannies are happy to accompany their employers on trips, and perceive it as a pleasant change from their normal routine. From an employer's point of view, having help on outings can make the day less tiring and more enjoyable.

When you're planning the outing, you need to think about how your nanny will feel about working alongside you, whether it will involve longer hours for her, and how you'll allocate responsibilities such as driving, making the picnic, and so on.

On the day, it's a good idea to discuss the structure of the day, agree who will keep an eye on specific children, and decide where you'll meet if you get separated.

The parent is usually in charge during an outing. Your nanny will normally defer to you, and you need to be specific about what you'd like her to do to prepare for the trip and on the day.

It is the employer's responsibility to meet all the nanny's expenses during the outing, including refreshments. This needn't extend to items from the gift shop, although it would be a nice gesture.

Based at home too

If you or your partner are based at home for part or all of the week, it is important to decide whether you really want your nanny to have sole charge of the children when you are around. If you are happy for her to have sole charge all the time, you will have to resist interfering with her daily plans and decisions. If you don't want her to have sole charge when you are around, you need to make it clear at her interview so that she can decide whether this is acceptable to her. Many nannies prefer to have sole charge, so if you are based at home try and think of other ways – shorter working hours, for example – of making the job attractive.

When you and the nanny are at home together, there can be a problem over the children playing each of you off against each other. If your nanny has sole charge all the time, you will need to defer to her during working hours. Ask the children to go to her with their requests, and back up her decisions even if you'd have given a different response. If she doesn't have sole charge, consult her on significant matters and try not to undermine her in front of the children.

You will have to ensure that your plans don't clash with your nanny's. Let her have your schedule in advance so that she knows when she needs to organise activities for the children and when you'd like to take responsibility for events. Consider using a joint diary to jot down things that you've both arranged to avoid 'double bookings'.

When you're around, your nanny may be less willing to take responsibility, which she should do if she has sole charge. Try stepping back a bit, so that she has to use her initiative and take control. If she doesn't have sole charge all the time, discuss with her what you'd like her to take responsibility for and what you'll do. After that, avoid doing her tasks unless she specifically asks for support and you're happy to help.

At times, you may feel that your home is being taken over by your nanny and her nanny friends during the day. Discuss your plans for the week with her in advance, and let her know when you'd like the house to yourself and when it would be suitable to invite other children to play.

HOW TO MANAGE THE BOUNDARIES BETWEEN YOUR NANNY AND OTHER STAFF AND RELATIVES

Sometimes you may have other people working, living or staying in your home. For example, you may employ a domestic cleaner or have a housekeeper as well as a nanny. You may also have relatives or friends who come to visit or who live with you. It is important that you clarify the boundaries between your nanny and any other staff you employ, so that each person knows what their responsibilities are, who they report to, and where overlaps may occur. You'll also need to ensure that your staff, relatives and other guests treat your nanny with respect.

The issues are similar for au pairs. Again, you'll need to establish clear boundaries between her and any other staff, and to ensure that your relatives and guests are kind to her.

ESTABLISHING GOOD BOUNDARIES BETWEEN YOUR NANNY AND OTHER STAFF

Staff	Tips for establishing good boundaries	Possible overlap with nanny
Maternity nurse/doula	• The maternity nurse's focus is on the new baby. She does all the nursery duties relating to the baby but not the other children. She gets up during the night to feed the baby if you wish. • A doula's role is to keep balance and harmony in the home when the mother has a baby. She will help with the baby, support the mother and try to keep the house in order. She will also occupy siblings, but if you have a nanny, ask the doula to focus on you, the baby and the house.	• Nursery duties for the new baby. • Looking after the new baby. • Occupying siblings (doula only). • Tidying up communal areas (doula only).
Domestic cleaner	• If you have a live-in nanny/au pair, ask your cleaner to clean her bedroom too, as this is a nice perk. • Ask the cleaner to hoover and dust the playroom and children's rooms. The nanny can keep them tidy. • Ask the nanny and cleaner to liaise about the best times for cleaning rooms, e.g., avoid cleaning the kitchen at mealtimes.	• Cleaning the children's rooms and playroom. • Children's ironing.

Staff	Tips for establishing good boundaries	Possible overlap with nanny
Housekeeper	• Housekeepers generally do the shopping, cleaning, cooking, mending and ironing. • The nanny should focus on looking after the children.	• Nursery duties. • Children's shopping and food. • Cleaning the children's rooms and playroom. • Washing and ironing for the children.
Au pair	• Au pairs often help with the children, do light housework, cleaning and ironing, baby-sitting and help at mealtimes. Generally speaking, an au pair is not supposed to be in sole charge for long periods, nor is she a domestic cleaner. They are meant to be given specific instructions about how to do tasks. • It is better if both the nanny and au pair report to you, rather than the au pair reporting to the nanny. • Try and divide their responsibilities clearly (e.g., who takes the children to school). Ask your nanny when	• Nursery duties. • Baby-sitting (possible overlap with live-in nanny). • Washing and ironing for the children. • Cooking for the children.

Staff	Tips for establishing good boundaries	Possible overlap with nanny
	she would like some extra help and ask the au pair to help her during busy times such as mornings during term-times. • Ask your au pair if she will help you at weekends, and give her at least two full days off during the week. • Ask each of them how they get on together. If conflicts arise, sort them out straight away.	
Gardener	• Taking care of the garden.	• Keeping an eye on the children when they are outside.

Resolving conflicts between staff

Sometimes there may be a clash of views between your nanny and the other staff you employ. If this occurs, you should try to resolve things straight away. Here are some tips for resolving conflicts between staff.

1. Talk to your nanny and the other member of staff separately. Ask each party for their view on what happened and how the situation could be resolved.
2. Then bring both parties together and ask them to share their view of the situation with each other. Ask each to summarise the other's point of view. Seek ideas about how the situation can be resolved.
3. Agree on a way forward, and then monitor progress and ask each of them how it is going.

Relatives and friends

From time to time relatives and guests will come to stay, or you may have a relative living with you permanently. Relatives and guests can interfere with a nanny's normal routine and make her life more complicated. They may also be critical of how she does her job and provide unsolicited advice and feedback to the parent, or, worse still, to the nanny herself.

If you have relatives or guests staying, or relatives offer to come and help for a specific reason – for instance, if you are going away and leaving the children with your nanny – discuss the issues and boundaries with your nanny.

During the discussion, be frank with her about your relatives' and guests' personalities, so that she can take them into consideration when considering their offer of help.

Ask her if she would like help, or if she would prefer to handle things alone. If she does want some help, ask her who could provide the best assistance and how.

Following the discussion, you need to make clear to your relatives and guests how you'd like them to help, and what is and isn't acceptable in terms of behaviour and feedback.

Employer perspective: Sent to India

'When I had my second baby, my mother-in-law, Yasmin, was very keen to come and help look after him. Yasmin made it clear that she wanted to act as maternity nurse, and did not want my nanny, Rachel, to interfere with what she was doing. I was concerned that Rachel would feel a bit bullied by her. She was a good nanny and I wanted her to stay for a long time. I spoke to Yasmin about the potential problem and she suggested that, as Rachel was interested in becoming a nursery teacher, we should pay for her to go out to India for a few months to work in a Montessori school in Delhi where we had contacts. I put the idea to Rachel. She was keen on the proposition and took us up on our offer. Yasmin moved in to look after the baby and take charge, and I bit my tongue!'

Employer perspective: Post-operative recovery

'Hilary looked after our four children under eight years old. Her days were very busy. When one of the boys, Tom, had his tonsils and adenoids out over the Easter holidays, I asked Hilary if she would like some help. Although I was able to take Tom into hospital, and be with him on the day of his operation, I had to work during the rest of the week and so I could not look after him during his convalescence. My husband could spend the night at the hospital, but also had to work that week.

'The two grandmothers kindly offered to come and stay to help out. Hilary knew them and said that she'd appreciate some assistance from them. I clarified what Hilary and the grandmothers' responsibilities would be. They would look after Tom – cook his meals and play games with him. Hilary would look after the other three children as normal, and she would bath Tom to save the grandmothers from having to do any heavy lifting. The arrangement worked well and we were all grateful for the extra help.'

ISSUES TO CONSIDER IF YOUR NANNY WANTS TO BRING HER BABY TO WORK

A nanny bringing her own child to your home can work well. However, it is an arrangement which needs to be thought through carefully, because there are both advantages and disadvantages.

NANNY BRINGING HER OWN CHILD TO WORK

Advantages	Disadvantages
If the nanny was with you before she became pregnant, the children have continuity of care.	Your children may come second to your nanny's children in an emergency or more generally.
The children have a baby to nurse.	Your nanny may take more time off work, e.g., if her baby is ill.
Your children have company.	You may have got beyond the baby phase and resent having to return to it.
It may reduce the intensity of your children's relationships with each other.	You may need to buy more equipment.
Your youngest child may be less spoilt.	Your nanny may be less flexible than previously, e.g. about baby-sitting.
Nannies who are mothers may be more empathetic about your role.	Your children may end up running errands for the nanny.
Day rates for nannies who bring their own baby to work are generally lower.	As a new mother, your nanny may have strong views about how to bring up children, which might contradict your own.

When a nanny brings her own child to work, the arrangement sometimes works well and sometimes doesn't. Those who have made things work suggest the following guidelines.

- You need to be very happy with your nanny's performance before you consider allowing her to bring her own child to work, because her doing so places extra burdens on you and your family.

- The nanny needs to be highly organised and punctual in order to manage the job and meet all the children's needs.
- If you are continuing to employ an existing nanny, you will need to re-contract with her, because she may not be able to work as many hours; for example, she may wish to work part-time, or evening baby-sitting may be more difficult. In addition, the daily pay rate for mothers bringing their children to work is generally less. Anticipate and discuss any concerns you may have, such as increased absenteeism when her child is sick.
- Agree a trial period. Review how the relationship is going on a weekly basis and be honest about your concerns.
- Ask your children for their views, both before the arrangement starts and once it is in place. They are the ones who are likely to gain or lose most from the situation.
- If it is not working, whether for you, for the nanny or for the children, terminate the arrangement. If your nanny has worked well in the past, it's better to maintain the happy memories, than to let the relationship turn sour.

There are some common teething problems with this arrangement.

WHEN NANNIES BRING THEIR CHILDREN TO WORK

Issues	Suggestions
My nanny is getting virtually free child care, while I'm paying for mine. She's with her children all the time, while I'm away from mine.	• Acknowledge your jealousy and resentment. • Remember that, in order to work for you, she's giving up time alone with her child.
I've noticed that my nanny isn't as strict with her baby as she was with mine. For example, her baby gets away with throwing its food on the floor.	• This is a common issue. It is often easier to discipline someone else's children than your own.

Issues	Suggestions
	• If you feel that the children are affected, ask her to apply one set of rules only, and give her some specific examples.
	• The upside is that your nanny may now be more sympathetic to your own attempts at discipline!
She takes time off to go to baby clinics.	• If your nanny works part-time, ask if she can do this in her own time.
	• Ask her to attend the clinics in your area, so that she can combine it with her normal child care duties.
I resent the fact that my children are asked to run errands for the nanny and her child.	• Ask the children if it bothers them. If not, forget it. Children often enjoy helping to look after little ones.
	• If it does bother them, ask her to restrict the errands to emergencies.
My nanny is absent more often, e.g., when her child is ill.	• Ask her to bring the baby to your house and nurse him/her there, as long as he/she isn't infectious. You could provide a travel cot.
	• Make it clear what is and isn't an acceptable level of absence during the year (e.g., up to five separate occasions of absence a year).

Employer perspective: And baby comes too

'Our daughters were at school full-time. They needed a nanny three days a week. The agency suggested a nanny on their books called Miriam, who was returning to work, having had a baby herself. We interviewed Miriam and liked her. However, we had some misgivings. Would her baby come first? Would our own children get enough attention? Was the house still safe enough for babies? We thought that we'd give the relationship a try and were amazed by its success.

'Two years on, Miriam was pregnant again. She worked up to her due date and returned to work after a short maternity leave with her second baby. Our daughters really enjoyed helping out with the new baby. They fought less, and when they needed peace and quiet (e.g., for homework), they retreated to their bedrooms. We felt that the arrangement had a positive impact on our daughters. Miriam gained because her baby and toddler had company and she could continue to work. It was a positive experience all round.'

HOW TO ORGANISE PROXY PARENTING

If you would like your nanny to carry out proxy parenting – that is, to look after your children on a twenty-four-hour basis – while you are away for a while, you need to ask her if she is willing and happy to do so. Even if she is, don't try it until you've considered the pros and cons.

The advantages for you are that you can spend time with your partner alone, or focus on work if you are away on a business trip. You can relax and catch up on your sleep and you may come back feeling refreshed. Proxy parenting can develop your nanny's skills, and often results in the children becoming closer to her. If she hasn't a child of her own, she may begin to appreciate what being a parent is like.

The disadvantages for you are that you may feel upset at leaving the children, and miss them while you're away. You may worry about being a long way from home if anything should happen to the children. When you return, you may feel jealous if any of the children are cooler towards you. There's also the fact that it costs more.

You'll also need to consider the pros and cons for your nanny and talk them over with her, especially if she hasn't cared for the children in this way before.

She may be glad to have the children in her sole charge for a while, and to be able to organise her time as she wishes – for instance, she won't be restricted by specific handover times. Children often behave better when their parents are away, and it can be fun for them as well as for her. There's also the fact that she'll be earning more.

On the other hand, she loses her free evenings, and may have disturbed nights. She may find the increased responsibility a burden, and be reluctant to take it on. The children may miss their parents and be upset. All these things mean that she may find proxy parenting very tiring and quite a challenge.

Before you go away

If your nanny agrees to do proxy parenting, there are several issues you will need to think through.

- How long you will be away, what additional hours she will have to work and how you will reward her (e.g., overtime, bonus, time off).
- What activities you are happy for her to undertake, and what she should avoid doing because it may be too stressful for her.
- Are there any activities you could organise (e.g., children's holiday clubs), which would occupy the children for a few hours and ease her burden?
- Do you need to organise any extra help to enable your nanny to have some free time (e.g., baby-sitters, relatives)?
- Who you will ask to support your nanny if there is an emergency. It should be someone who lives locally.
- If you have an option, when is the best time to go from her

viewpoint? In the school holidays, when things are more relaxed, or during term-time, when the children are more occupied during the day? Just after she's had a holiday so that she's feeling refreshed, or just before her holiday, so that she can recuperate afterwards?

- How will you prepare the children for your departure?
- How much will you provide as a 'float' for outings?

Discuss and agree with your nanny the timing of the cover, hours, pay, activities and additional support. Before you leave, give her your telephone number and the number of the person she can call in an emergency.

While you are away

Telephone her regularly, to check how everything is going and to speak to the children. When you're buying presents for the children, don't forget a gift for your nanny as well.

When you get back

First of all, thank your nanny for her flexibility. Review how it went, and ask her what went well and what went less well. Also, find out if there is anything that you should do differently next time, or anything that she has learnt from the experience. Check how tired she is, and give her some time off, if possible, to recuperate.

SUMMARY

- Employer–nanny relationships are more emotional and intense than other social and work relationships.
- It is important to establish and manage the boundaries of your relationship with your nanny or au pair.
- Don't attempt too much intimacy with your nanny. It is more difficult to manage someone if you are very close to them.
- It is normal to be jealous of your nanny at times. Acknowledge your jealousy and, unless it is making you unhappy, move on.
- When you and your nanny are looking after the children together, agree your responsibilities.
- If you employ other staff, identify any potential overlaps in responsibilities and clarify who should do what.
- If you have relatives or guests living or staying with you, protect your nanny from interference and unsolicited feedback.
- If your nanny is pregnant and wants to bring her baby to work, weigh up the pros and cons carefully. Each situation is different.
- When organising proxy parenting, discuss and agree the hours, pay, activities and additional support before you leave. Keep in regular contact while you're away, and on your return, review how it went.

Part IV:

Managing Your Changing Needs

12 Handling Child Care as Your Needs Change

'She wants to reduce her hours when all three children are at school, but she will still collect them and work in the holidays.' – Mum

'I have recently found a male au pair who loves playing football with the children and is very practical around the house.' – Mum

As your children get older and enter full-time education, your child-care needs will change. You may want to keep employing your current nanny, but on a different basis. In practice, this often isn't feasible because many nannies are not happy to change their duties (for example, to take on household tasks), or to have their salary reduced. Unless you are prepared to be very flexible, you may need to recruit a new person to meet your changed needs.

In this section we outline five different types of flexible child-care arrangements for school-age children. You need to weigh up the advantages and issues of each, and consider which one would best suit your family and financial circumstances.

REASONS FOR CHANGING YOUR CHILD-CARE ARRANGEMENTS

In our survey, we asked employers and nannies why child-care arrangements might change and nannies might eventually leave their current jobs. In the majority of cases, the reason was the children moving into full-time education and the job becoming less interesting for the nanny.

In addition, your children's needs change and they may require a nanny with different skills. Some nannies are fantastic with babies but less suitable for older children. For example, school-age boys may benefit from having a male student or au pair to look after them.

As your children get older, you may require help early in the mornings for the school runs; after school and in the early evenings for support with homework; during the school holidays; and for emergencies such as when the children are sick.

Some parents decide to change their own working or social arrangements so that they can cover these times. But for many parents, this is not an option.

ADVANTAGES AND DISADVANTAGES OF CHANGING YOUR NANNY

Generally speaking, a good nanny is worth trying to keep. Think about your changing requirements and ask her whether she would be prepared to do different hours and/or duties in order to accommodate you. If she would be, you are very fortunate. (Don't forget to issue her with a new written contract of employment which reflects the changes.)

In practice, it may not be easy to negotiate a change to your nanny's terms and conditions. For example, familiarity may result in your nanny being less flexible about what she's prepared to do in the home to occupy herself.

If your current nanny does not wish to change her working arrangements, or if you feel that she cannot adequately meet your changed requirements, it is time to recruit a new nanny. In most cases this is what happens.

Although the change is uncomfortable in the short term, in the long term you may well benefit. You can recruit a nanny whose specific skills match your children's requirements and who will fully meet your needs, and she should be completely comfortable with

RETAINING YOUR NANNY

Advantages	Disadvantages
You keep someone who is good and whom you like.	Your nanny is likely to be less flexible and accommodating than someone recruited to meet your new needs.
You ensure continuity and security for the children.	She may look back longingly to the old arrangements.
You are familiar with your nanny's personality, personal needs and how to manage her.	Your existing nanny's skills may not suit your children's current needs.
You don't experience the discomfort of change.	Over the years, you may have lost the initiative in your relationship, and it may not be easy to get what you need out of your negotiations with her.
You are saved the expense and time of recruiting a new nanny.	It can be expensive keeping a nanny, because over time her salary increases may push her salary over market rates.
	It might not work out, which could spoil your good relationship.

the arrangements. You have a new, enthusiastic employee who is keen to make things work, and you part from your old nanny on excellent terms and remember the good times.

CHILD-CARE ARRANGEMENTS FOR SCHOOL-AGE CHILDREN

There are various types of flexible child-care arrangements which you can organise to suit your needs. We have identified five options, and list the advantages and issues associated with each, together with tips for making them work.

Flexible-hours agreements

A flexible-hours agreement is an attractive option if you wish to keep your current nanny, because it means that you can continue to pay a good wage, but have cover when you need it.

In our survey, 34 per cent of nannies said they wanted shorter working hours, so this arrangement might suit some of them. A flexible-hours agreement aims to reduce a nanny's working hours during termtime, while providing good cover during holidays and in emergencies. There are a number of different approaches to flexible hours, and we give two examples.

An annual hours agreement

You need to work out what hours you need your nanny to work during termtime and the school holidays. It is better to ask for more hours than you need, and let your nanny go early occasionally, than to ask her to exceed her hours on a regular basis.

For example, in termtime you may ask for cover:

Termtime	Holidays
7.30–9.30 am 3.00–8.00 pm	7.30 am–6.30 pm
Total termtime hours	*Total holiday hours*
7 hours per day	11 hours per day

With this arrangement, your nanny is likely to be doing a 35-hour working week during termtime and a 55-hour working week during the holidays. You pay her the same each week. Over the year, the length of her average working week will be less than the 50 hours specified in her contract, so there will be some 'spare hours' which you can use for emergencies, baby-sitting or proxy parenting.

ANNUAL HOURS AGREEMENT CALCULATION

Assumptions

50-hour working week (live-out standard week), e.g., a 10-hour working day for 5 days a week.

4 weeks' holiday a year, plus 8 bank holidays. In total, 28 days' paid holiday.

Three school terms of 11 weeks (taking out one week from each for half-term), i.e., 33 weeks of school.

The cover required being 7.30–9.30am and 3.00–8.00 pm (i.e., 7 hours a day) during termtime; and 7.30am–6.30pm (i.e., 11 hours) during the school holidays.

Working hours available during the year

Total hours in a year: 50 (hours a week) × 52 (weeks a year) = 2600 hours

Holidays = 10 (average hours a day) × 28 (total days holiday) = 280 hours

Total hours available: 2600 (hours in a year) – 280 (hours of holiday) = 2320 hours

Cover required

Termtime

7 (hours each day) × 5 (days a week) × 33 (weeks at school each year) = 1155 hours

School holidays

11 (hours a day) × 5 (days a week) x 19 (weeks' school holiday) = 1045 hours

Minus nanny's holiday

10 (hours a day average) × 28 (total days' holiday) = 280 hours

Total cover required

1155 (termtime hours) + 1045 (holiday hours) – 280 (nanny's holiday hours) = 1920 hours

'Spare hours' available

2320 (total hours available) – 1920 (total cover required) = 400 'spare hours' available

If you require more spare hours, you need to agree this with your nanny and pay her some overtime.

ANNUAL HOURS AGREEMENT

Advantages	Disadvantages
You get good cover when you need it.	The arrangement is complex to explain.
Your nanny can maintain her normal salary.	You need to calculate and agree the 'spare hours' remaining.
You have 'spare hours' for extra requirements, e.g., baby-sitting.	It may involve early starts and late finishes for your nanny.
Your nanny is free during the day in termtime, but must be available to provide cover for emergencies at short notice. She could take a college course, which some nannies in our survey wanted to do.	Your nanny might leave at the start of the holidays and, unless you'd held back some pay, you'd lose out. If she gets another job during the day, she may be tired and less flexible.

Some tips for making this arrangement work:

- Give your nanny a mobile or a bleeper to ensure that you can contact her during emergencies, for example, if your child becomes ill while at school.
- Pay her the same salary throughout the year but keep some salary back, or pay a bonus, to motivate her to stay during the holidays.
- Provide a note of the 'spare hours' remaining on her payroll slip each week, or agree them with her once a month.

- Pay a good wage to start with for the flexible agreement, to compensate for the early starts and late finishes.
- Don't always feel that you need to use up all the 'spare hours' each year. It's a bonus for her if you don't.

A two-tier pay agreement

Another way of ensuring that you have flexible cover during termtime and holidays is to pay your nanny at two different rates: a higher one when she's looking after your children, and a lower one when she is not. The lower rate acts as a 'retainer'. For example, you could pay her the normal hourly rate when she's with the children and half that rate when she's not looking after them.

Termtime cover	Rate
8.00–9.30 am	£6.00 per hour
9.30am–3.00pm	£3.00 per hour
3.00pm–6.00pm	£6.00 per hour

Holiday or sickness cover	
8.00am–6.00pm	£6.00 per hour

This would involve your nanny taking a drop in salary, but the decrease would be less than if you paid her for the actual hours worked. Some nannies like to work reduced hours as their personal circumstances change, and these nannies may be quite happy with this type of arrangement.

A TWO-TIER PAY AGREEMENT

Advantages	Disadvantages
It's simple to administer. You have a nanny who will cover termtime and holidays, and is available when you need her in an emergency, e.g., sickness. She is free to do as she likes with the free time and is actually being paid something for it. You pay as you go, so if your nanny leaves you halfway through the year, she would not owe you any time.	Your nanny would not earn as much as she would for a normal 50-hour week, which may be an issue for some nannies. She may get another job during the day. This may make it more difficult for her to respond quickly to your needs in an emergency.

Some tips for making this arrangement work:

- During your nanny's holidays, pay her at least an average weekly rate so as to avoid any resentment.
- Provide her with a mobile phone or bleeper, to ensure that you can contact her during emergencies.
- This arrangement may be particularly popular with more mature nannies who have their own accommodation and would like time off for domestic chores, etc.

Nanny/housekeepers

If you want to occupy a nanny on a full-time basis when the children are at school, you can combine nannying and housekeeping tasks. Some nannies are more flexible than others about doing domestic chores such as family washing and ironing, cleaning, shopping and cooking. If you are at home and you do not need someone to take sole charge, you could employ a mother's help instead of a nanny/housekeeper.

The main advantages of having a nanny/housekeeper are that you may be able to keep a good nanny if she is flexible, and ensure continuity for the children; you might be pampered (your meals prepared, etc.) by your nanny during termtime; and you could end up paying less for for domestic help during termtime.

But there may be disadvantages, too. Good nannies do not necessarily make good housekeepers, and many nannies resent being asked to carry out household tasks. In the school holidays, the domestic chores will probably not get done. It is a more expensive option than employing a nanny on a part-time basis; and if your nanny leaves, you've lost your domestic help too.

If the relationship is to work, you must be quite clear about what you expect to be done on a weekly basis. Provide a job description, outlining the key tasks, both domestic and nannying. You will need to be flexible about the housekeeping if there is an emergency such as a child being off school sick, and also stipulate that the child has priority. Discuss what housekeeping tasks, if any, could still be done during the school holidays, and organise additional help if necessary.

Nanny-share arrangements

You could organise, or ask your nanny to fix up, a nanny-share arrangement so that your nanny is still fully occupied and remunerated.

The main advantages of using a nanny-share arrangement to provide flexible cover are that you keep a good nanny and your nanny maintains her salary level, and in some cases earns more. Also, your children may enjoy mixing with the other children in the share.

There are drawbacks, too. Your nanny might end up having to work harder for the same pay, and might resent it. During the holidays she will have her hands full, which might affect what your children can do. You may have other children using your home, and they might be noisy and messy or your own children may be at home less, which they may resent. Your nanny will report to other people, too, and you'll have to take their needs into consideration, so you'll have less control. Lastly, it may be quite tiring for your nanny.

We advise you to try and give your nanny additional money for taking on the nanny share, so that she doesn't resent the additional responsibility and hassle.

Employer perspective: The nanny-share register saves Ros's job

'I had had a nanny, Ros, for three years. She'd looked after my daughter, Victoria, from birth. When Victoria started going to a local nursery, I wanted to keep employing Ros, but I couldn't afford her salary plus the nursery school fees. I needed help in the mornings before nursery and from noon onwards. I read about a nanny-share register in a local magazine and I rang up. I contacted a number of families on the register and found one that interested me. The family had a six-month-old baby and wanted morning cover from 9.15am until 1.00pm. I discussed the family with Ros. She felt that she could manage the extra commitment. Ros and I met the parents and the baby, and discussed how the arrangement might work. We decided that Ros would spend the mornings at the baby's house and the afternoons at my house. Ros liked her new job, because she was now fully occupied, she had a baby to look after again and her salary increased by 10 per cent. I was happy because I was able to keep my nanny and I didn't have to pay for full-time child care.'

Au pairs

As your children grow older, you may need someone with different skills to look after them. Older children require someone who is organised and punctual for the school runs and after-school activities, who can help them with their homework, and who is good company and can organise fun outings during the holidays. A good, bright au pair may be able to meet your child-care needs instead of a nanny.

If you are not around all the time, and the au pair will be in sole charge of your children, you will need to recruit an au pair with previous experience of looking after children, and someone with good references.

One advantage of having an au pair is that it is cheaper. In addition, highly educated au pairs can make stimulating companions for your children. Au pairs become part of the family and can provide very flexible help, including time over the weekend (if they are given time off during the week to compensate) and help on holiday if necessary.

The disadvantages are that au pairs normally work a 25-hour week, so you may need some additional cover during the school holidays. They often have little experience of looking after children, and their main motivation for working may be to visit England and to learn English. Au pairs often don't stay very long.

If you are replacing your nanny with an au pair, bear in mind the following:

- You are more likely to find an au pair with child-care experience if you recruit one who has already spent some time in the UK with a family. It makes checking references easier too.
- If you have boys or feisty girls, there are some male au pairs who might be good companions for them.
- You will need to provide more input on how to manage the children than you would for a trained nanny. Expect to spend more time with an au pair in the evenings and at weekends.

Host-family perspective: Scaling down child care

'I gave up my job when I was expecting twins. At first I needed a lot of help and had a full-time nanny. However, when the twins started nursery, I felt that I didn't need a nanny any more. When my nanny handed in her notice, I decided to find an au pair instead. It was a cheaper option and, as I was at home, I could provide guidance on what the au pair should do. I went through an international agency and chose Elena.

'Elena fitted in well. She was particularly good at playing with the children, walking to and from the nursery with Alex and Freddy, and mucking in at weekends and on holidays. She wasn't very good at cooking – everything came out burnt – and so I did the cooking and Elena entertained the children. Both of us were happy with the arrangement.'

Part-time nannies

You could employ a nanny on a part-time basis to meet your child-care needs. She might be a nanny who wants to work fewer hours, a student with previous child-care experience, or a nanny with her own child. If your current nanny's circumstances change – for example, if she gets married or starts her own family – she might be interested in continuing to work for you on a part-time basis, thus providing continuity of care for the children.

It is a relatively inexpensive option, because you only pay for the cover you receive. Furthermore, nannies who bring their children to work generally charge less.

However, it may not be easy to find someone who wishes to work part-time, solely for you. A part-time nanny may not want to start early or finish late, and she may not want to work extended hours during the holidays. If you use a student, the arrangement may not last long, because she may not be able to continue working for you after she has finished the course.

Many part-time nanny arrangements work well. Some tips for ensuring that yours does are:

- Be clear about your child-care needs, and be generous in your estimate of the hours you require during the school holidays.
- If you wouldn't be happy if your nanny took on another part-time job, explain this to her at the outset of the arrangement.
- You may need additional support if your nanny's flexibility is limited, for instance, if she can't baby-sit in the evenings because she is a single mother.

- Employing a nanny with her own baby can work well, but think through the advantages and disadvantages in advance.

Employer perspective: Part-time help

'I worked for three days a week as a GP in a country practice. In the past, I had employed nannies to look after my children, but when they all went to school I no longer needed full-time help. It was wonderful to reclaim my house and not have anyone living in. I recruited a part-time nanny called Jo. I needed someone to pick the boys up from school in the afternoons, give them a snack and encourage them to do their homework. I got home at around 7.30 pm. The arrangement suited Jo well; she was studying to be a teacher at a local college and was free in the late afternoons, early evenings and school holidays. I soon realised that Jo was a good cook and I asked her if she'd be willing to do additional cooking, in particular, to prepare the evening meal for us on the days that she worked. Jo loved cooking and agreed to do so. This arrangement worked well because it enabled me to spend more time with my children after work.'

SUMMARY

- As the children get older and enter full-time education, your child-care needs will change.
- You need to discuss your changing needs with your nanny, and see if she is willing to alter her hours and/or responsibilities to accommodate you. If she is, you will need to agree a new contract of employment with her.
- In the majority of cases, parents tend to start afresh, and enter into different child-care arrangements.
- There are many different types of child-care arrangements for school-age children. Each has its own advantages and drawbacks. You need to weigh up which arrangement will suit you best.

13 Ensuring Happy Endings

How I Felt when my Nanny left

'I felt very, very sad when she left because I loved her so much.' – *Child*

'She was with us for two years and she is now a good friend of the family.' – *Mum*

'I still write to my old family and send photos to them and gifts.' – *Au pair*

All carer relationships have a beginning and an end. At some point, however difficult and traumatic it may be, you and your nanny or au pair will separate.

CONQUERING THE FEAR OF ENDINGS

Ending relationships is a painful business. If you really like your nanny or au pair, and have been together a while, it can be hard to envisage life without her. Even if you feel that it is time to make a change, it can still be difficult to broach the subject.

When you ask your nanny or au pair to leave, or your nanny or au pair tells you that she wants to move on, you may experience a sense of loss and a fear of what the future will bring. These feelings are completely normal. The diagram entitled 'The loss curve' illustrates the types of feelings people have when faced with change. Generally speaking, the feelings are more intense the first time it happens, and when you separate from someone who has been with you for a long time, as illustrated by the employers' and nannies' stories.

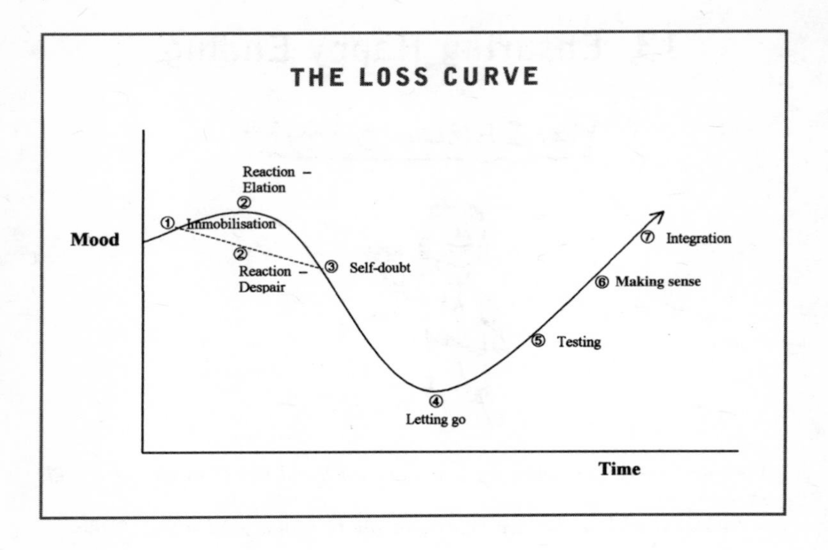

Key

(1) Immobilisation: shock and disbelief; feeling that you can't understand it.
(2) Reaction: can be either elation or despair.
(3) Self-doubt: anxiety, anger and sadness. You can feel very critical. (Sometimes individuals move from immobilisation to self-doubt without feeling either elation or despair in between.)
(4) Letting go: feeling that what has happened has happened, and that you have to move forward from this low point.
(5) Testing: exploring options and starting to look to the future.
(6) Making sense of it: what have you survived in the past? What will life look like beyond?
(7) Integration: acceptance of loss, saying goodbye and moving on.

Employer perspective: Losing my first nanny

'I organised a nanny-share arrangement with another family. We recruited Sally together and were very pleased with her. She was very good at looking after babies and pleasant to have around the house. Unexpectedly, I found that I was pregnant again when my son was only eight months old. After a few weeks, I told the other mother and we agreed that we'd like Sally to continue to look after our two children (who were both under two years old) and the new baby. I spoke to Sally about it. Sally was unsure that she could manage three young children. She offered to work for me. I wanted to continue the nanny share because the children got on well and we couldn't afford to employ our own live-out nanny.

'On the morning of my son's first birthday party, Sally gave me one month's notice. I felt devastated by the news. We'd anticipated that Sally would stay another eight months, until I had had the new baby and returned to work. Sally had only completed nine months of her contract with us. I walked around London doing the birthday shopping feeling very low. My son, Sam, and I liked Sally and would miss her. I also felt angry about the timing of the announcement. I had expected Sam's first birthday to be very joyous, but it was hard to put on a brave face. The birthday party felt like a sombre event, but it was also the lowest moment.

'As each day passed, I got used to the idea that Sally was leaving and accepted it. Our plans also changed. We decided to move to a larger house to accommodate our growing family. This meant that we'd have enough room for a live-in nanny. A live-in nanny could work more flexible hours and I could afford to employ her by myself in the future, once the baby had arrived. In addition, I had come round to Sally's view that three children under three were too much for one nanny to cope with. Sally's departure was initially a real blow to me, but it did provide an opportunity to reflect upon what I needed, and to recruit a new nanny to meet our changed requirements. Sally and I parted on good terms and Sally has remained a friend of the family.'

Over the years we have employed quite a lot of nannies, and we always feel sad saying goodbye to them, but also optimistic about the future. Each new nanny brings her own different and special skills. After the first few weeks, we've been pleased with our choice of new nanny.

You may also experience a sense of loss when an au pair leaves, particularly if you have got on well and she has become a friend of the family.

Parents often put up with all sorts of unnecessary aggravation – for example, hours that don't suit them, inflated rates of pay, or an uncomfortable atmosphere at home – because they can't bear to part from their nanny or au pair. Some nannies also dislike change and so stay longer than they should, because they prefer to stick with the familiar. If you are in this situation, we would encourage you to face it and to make a change. The initial conversation is always the worst part, and after that both the parent and nanny can start to look ahead.

WHY NANNIES AND AU PAIRS LEAVE

Employer's and host family's perspectives

From the employer's perspective, reasons that you might wish to change your nanny include:

- The children no longer need full-time care and your nanny does not wish to do household tasks or work part-time.
- Your children require someone with different skills.
- You feel that you have become too close and lost the initiative in the relationship and you'd like to make a fresh start with a new nanny.
- You are stopping work and no longer want help with child care.
- You realise that the relationship has run its course, and you need a change.
- Your nanny is not performing well, despite feedback and coaching from you.
- Serious or gross misconduct.

From the host family's perspective, the most common reasons why an au pair leaves include:

- Her visa expiring.
- She is not suited to housework and looking after children.
- A personality clash and/or she is too moody.
- We no longer need an au pair, because the children are older.

Nanny's and au pair's perspectives

In our survey we asked nannies why they expected that they would eventually leave. Their responses, in descending order of frequency, were:

- The children are in full-time education and/or they no longer need me.
- To have my own children.
- I need a more challenging job/I need longer hours.
- To pursue a different career.
- To travel/return home/move location.
- The hours are too long/exhaustion.
- To have sole charge of the children.
- To look after a baby again.
- To get married.
- Expiry of my contract.
- For more money.
- My boss is stopping work/working from home, and no longer needs help.
- To get a live-out job (live-in nannies).

Reasons au pairs gave for leaving their host families were:

- Visa expiring.
- To work fewer hours and/or get more pocket money.
- To do less housework.
- Feeling very homesick and/or lonely.
- To have more privacy.
- To have more contact with a family and to speak more English.
- To travel.

Occasionally, a nanny or au pair leaves with no notice and little explanation. For example, a live-out nanny doesn't turn up after the weekend, or a live-in nanny or au pair doesn't come downstairs one morning, and when you go to find her, her room has been cleared. When this happens, you may experience shock and disbelief that someone can treat you like this. If you can, contact her and ask her why she's left. It is important to know what part, if any, you played in her decision to leave: there may be lessons that you can learn for next time. In some cases nannies and au pairs have been enticed back, either permanently, on different terms, or else for a short period until the employer finds a replacement.

Host-family perspective: The empty bedroom syndrome

'I was a single mother and had employed au pairs for many years to help around the house and to provide cover while I was working (once my children were at school). I'd had some excellent au pairs over the years who had become family friends. We'd even been to visit a couple of them in their home countries, Poland and Spain.

'One day, I returned home early to collect the children from school. I went to my au pair's room to speak to her, and found that it was empty. I was shocked and angry. I couldn't understand how someone could do this to me. I wanted to find my au pair, Viola. I drove to her friend's house. I was lucky: Viola was there. I confronted her and asked her what she was intending to do and why. Viola explained that she felt homesick and had booked a flight home the following day. I empathised with Viola, but also explained how upset I was because she hadn't given me any time to make other arrangements and I had no cover. I was working on a big contract for a client and I'd let the client down if I couldn't work. I begged Viola to reconsider and to stay a bit longer, and I offered her some extra cash. Eventually, Viola agreed to change her ticket and to stay for another few weeks until I could find a replacement.'

STEPS FOR PARTING ON GOOD TERMS

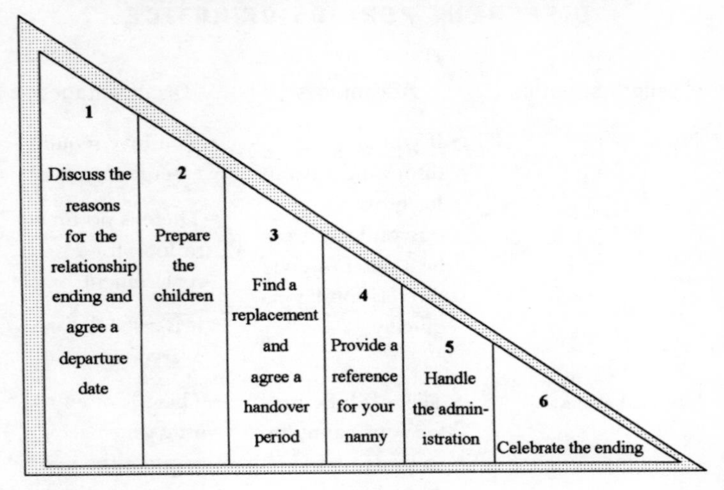

Step 1: Discuss the reasons for the relationship ending, and agree a departure date

Whether you are instigating the change or your nanny or au pair wants to move on, have an open and honest discussion about the reasons. See if anything can be done to salvage the situation, and, if not, discuss an appropriate notice period and a departure date.

Employer's or host family's decision

If you are asking your nanny or au pair to leave for performance related reasons, be honest about it. Her response is likely to be defensive and she may be angry. Allow her some time and space to think the situation over, and be available for further discussions. With nannies, if you think that the atmosphere at home is going to be tense, agree the minimum notice period in her contract or ask her to go sooner and pay her in lieu of notice.

If the reason you are parting with your nanny or au pair is not performance-related, it is likely to be a more comfortable departure. You should give her as much notice as possible, so that she can find another job.

DIFFERENT PERIODS OF NOTICE

Length of notice	Advantages	Disadvantages
None	• If you are dismissing a nanny for gross misconduct, it can be a relief to end the relationship quickly.	• You may require emergency cover. • There is no time to look for a replacement. • It is a shock for everyone.
Under 4 weeks	• There is little time for your nanny or au pair to wind down before she leaves.	• There is often too little time to organise the right replacement unless you're lucky. • There may not be enough time for you all to get used to the idea of change.
4–8 weeks	• This is usually enough time to recruit a replacement. • It leaves you all enough time to get used to the idea of separation.	• You may lose your nanny earlier if she's on 4 weeks' notice. • Your nanny may start to wind down early.
8 weeks and over	• You all have plenty of time to get used to the idea of separation.	• You may lose your nanny earlier if she has a job offer in the meantime.

Length of notice	Advantages	Disadvantages
	• There is plenty of time to recruit a replacement. • It is useful if you are trying to recruit from a specific source (e.g., a specialist college) or to recruit a nanny or au pair from overseas.	• Your nanny may start to wind down early. • You may not find it easy to recruit someone more than 2 months ahead.

Nanny or au pair's decision

If your nanny hands in her notice, or your au pair tells you she wishes to leave, earlier than you expected her to, it is important to understand her reasons for wishing to move on. Try and listen objectively to her point of view, and summarise what she says to ensure you've understood it. If you would like her to stay, ask her what needs to happen for her to change her mind.

If you cannot persuade her to stay, let her go gracefully. Negotiate a reasonable notice period which leaves you enough time to recruit the right replacement – at least two months is ideal for both nannies and au pairs. Nearer the time of her departure, carry out an 'exit interview'. Ask her:

- Her full reasons for wanting to leave.
- What she's liked about the job.
- What aspects she's enjoyed less.
- What would make the job more attractive for the next incumbent.
- What she has liked about the way you've managed her.
- What you should do differently.

The exit interview can provide useful information, which you can use when recruiting, and managing her replacement.

Severance pay and bonus payments (nannies only)

When the nanny is leaving at their request, some employers provide severance pay in addition to notice, to cushion her between jobs. The normal rate is one week's pay for each year of service. If the nanny is instigating the change, it is not normal to pay her severance pay. However, if she has been with the family for a long time, it is customary to give her a generous gift.

If you are concerned that your nanny may leave before you are ready to lose her, you could offer her a bonus if she stays until a specified date. For example, if she stays until all the children have gone back to school in September, you will give her an extra week's salary.

Step 2: Prepare the children

The next step is for you and your nanny or au pair to discuss how you prepare the children for the change, to agree what you will say and when; and what level of contact your nanny or au pair wishes to have, once she's left.

We have found that it is helpful to hint, when you see the change coming, that your nanny will not stay for ever. Ask her to prepare the children in this way, too. Nearer her date of departure, and before you start recruiting a replacement, tell the children that she is moving on and why. Ask her to reinforce the message to the children and to reassure them that she will keep in touch with them.

Encourage your children to discuss their feelings – by saying things like 'It'll be sad when Laura leaves won't it?'. But don't create despair where none exists. If the children are taking the nanny's imminent departure calmly, go with it. Children can sometimes accept change more easily than we can.

As au pairs tend to be with their families for shorter periods, the children may adjust more quickly to their departure, and even become used to it as they get older. However, it is still important to prepare the children for the change.

Step 3: Find a replacement and agree a handover period

This can take a lot of time and energy. It involves thinking through what type of child care you are going to need in the future; contacting agencies and placing advertisements; sifting applications; preparing for interviews; interviewing; evaluating candidates, and making a decision and an offer.

It is good practice to involve your departing nanny in the recruitment process. You can do this by seeking her views on the job; asking her to spend time with each interviewee; getting her views about candidates, once they have left; and arranging a handover period of at least a couple of days. Involving her in the process helps her to get used to the idea that she's leaving, gives you the benefit of her intuition on a replacement, and will save you time at the induction stage.

You can also involve your current au pair in recruiting your next au pair, if they speak the same language. For example, some host families ask their departing au pair to ring up the new au pair, to tell her about your family and the situation and to assess how much child-care experience she has. In addition, they may ask their departing au pair to write a letter welcoming the new one. The letter usually describes her responsibilities and explains what the family is like. This can help the new au pair to settle in more quickly.

If your current nanny or au pair is leaving for performance-related reasons, you may prefer not to include her in the recruitment of her successor, and to avoid a handover period.

Step 4: Provide a written reference for your nanny or au pair

You will be expected to provide your nanny or au pair with a written reference. It is relatively easy to do if you think she is good and can enthuse about her skills.

However, if you are not pleased with some aspects of your nanny's or au pair's performance, writing a reference is more tricky. The protocol is to write a reference stating what she is good at and to leave out her weaknesses, unless you feel that they might endanger others. If you consider that she was extremely poor in most respects, you could refuse to provide a reference. Example references for a good and a poor nanny are given in Appendix VI.

Do not be tempted to lie for an easy life; it is not fair to other employers or host families, and you wouldn't like someone to do it to you. Good nanny and au pair agencies follow up references and ask questions to elicit how good the nanny or au pair really is, and sensible parents do the same.

Once you have written the reference, give it to your nanny or au pair and ask her how happy she is with it. If she seems disappointed, discuss the matter with her. It may be a language issue. For example, you may use the word 'professional' as the highest form of praise, but she may interpret it as meaning 'technically competent, but cold'. If you can see her point of view, be prepared to amend the reference. However, don't write anything that you know is misleading or untrue.

Some families ask their nanny or au pair to write a reference for them, too. This can be used to inform agencies, candidates and your new nanny or au pair what you're like to work for.

Step 5: Handle the administration

When your nanny leaves, there are always some administrative details that need to be sorted out. In particular you will need to:

- Calculate how much you owe your nanny in wages, unused holiday, severance pay and/or bonus payments.
- Calculate any debts (e.g., phone bills or loans) that she has outstanding, and deduct them from your final payment to her. Let her know what her final payment will be and explain the calculation. Check that she is happy with it.
- Make a final payment to the tax office for her tax and National Insurance. Complete the P12 and send it off.
- Transfer names on any benefits that you provide (e.g., car insurance, car breakdown cover, sports club membership, telephone line).

With au pairs, you need to pay any outstanding pocket money and deduct any money that she owes you.

Step 6: Celebrate the Ending

It is very important to celebrate the ending of your relationship so that the parting is as happy as possible, and leaves you all with good memories.

You will need to plan in advance what you are going to do. Typical activities during the last few days include taking your nanny or au pair out for a farewell meal; having a party for her at home and inviting her friends; giving her a card (perhaps made by the children) and a gift; and saying goodbye when she actually leaves.

We have celebrated quite a few endings between us, and have a few recommendations. Be generous with your gift: buy your nanny or au pair something special, so that she has a constant reminder of her happy time with you. Discuss with her when you will telephone and/or see her again.

In the case of nannies, it's a good idea to involve your new one in the celebrations if you are having a handover period. The children will be more comfortable if they get to know the new nanny while they still have the security of their old nanny's presence. Try to spare your new nanny the awkwardness of witnessing the final goodbye. It can be embarrassing for her, and it may stop you all expressing what you want to.

Employer perspective: Farewell to Harriet

'Harriet had been with us for five years as a daily nanny. She looked after our three children, Jenny (6), Robert (4) and Jack (1). Harriet was pregnant and leaving to have her own baby. We were delighted for her, but also sad to see her go. We decided to take her out to a restaurant for lunch to celebrate her time with us. We asked her if she'd like to bring her partner too, and she said that she would. The children were very involved in planning the event. They chose the restaurant, made cards, selected some presents to give to her during lunch and made a cake. The meal was a great success.

It was a really joyful occasion, and a great way to end five happy years together.'

DEALING WITH THE LOSS

The first few weeks after a nanny or au pair has left are the worst in terms of missing her. Initially, the children may be quieter and more withdrawn, and they may cry for her. You yourself may miss your ex-nanny or old au pair, if you had become friends. At the same time, both you and the children are having to deal with the discomfort of getting used to a new nanny or au pair.

Some tips for dealing with the loss in the first few weeks are:

- Allow the children to cry, and comfort them. Talk about how they are feeling and say it is okay to feel sad.
- Be sensitive to the new nanny's or au pair's needs. Try not to mention your ex-nanny or old au pair all the time, or put her on a pedestal so that your new nanny or au pair feels that she can never match up to her. Do not complain about your ex-nanny or old au pair either, as it is unprofessional.
- After a week, telephone your ex-nanny or old au pair to see how she is getting on. Get your children to talk to her and express their feelings.
- If your ex-nanny or au pair is still in the neighbourhood, and it upsets your children when they bump into her, agree to use different playgroups for a few weeks, until the children have adjusted to your new nanny.
- If your ex-nanny wants to come back and visit, and you feel it is too soon, ask her to wait a few weeks, to let the children get over her departure before they see her again.

As the weeks go by, the feeling of loss wears off. When it feels right, you can invite your ex-nanny back for a visit. We recommend that you ask her to visit over the weekend, when you are around, so that you are there to comfort the children if they get upset when she leaves again. Furthermore, a weekend visit reinforces the idea that your ex-nanny is no longer the children's nanny but a family friend.

Keep in touch with your ex-nanny and invite her to family events such as birthday parties. However, do be sensitive to your current nanny's feelings on this issue. Discuss your plans with her, and only go ahead if she is happy and you feel that the children won't play up for her after spending time at the weekend with their old nanny.

Host families can keep in touch with their old au pair, by inviting her to visit them again, by travelling to her country to visit her, and by exchanging letters and e-mails and remembering her birthday.

Employer perspective: A painful separation

'Emma had been with us for three years as a live-in nanny. We were all very fond of her – she had become part of the family. Emma was particularly close to our middle son, Paul, whom she'd looked after since he was six months old. The decision to separate was mutual. Emma wanted to buy her own flat and be a live-out nanny, and I felt that it was time for a change. She was an excellent nanny who would be hard to replace. We agreed a five-month notice period, which gave us both plenty of time to get used to the idea. Emma and I both told the children – hinting at first and then, as the departure date got nearer, being quite explicit about her going.

'I recruited a new nanny, Anne. She was completely different to Emma, which helped, because the children didn't compare them. Anne had a degree and experience working in a nursery but she'd never been a nanny. She wanted to work for a family before taking a teaching diploma with a view to becoming an educational psychologist. Anne had lots of energy and the children liked her. I organised a two-day handover period and planned a lunch and other activities to celebrate Emma's departure. The children made Emma some cards and we bought her a television for her new flat. On the day that Emma left, it was very difficult to say goodbye. We all cried a lot. Our new nanny, Anne, watched in horror as we waved Emma off, all wailing loudly. In retrospect, we should have spared her that. That evening when I went upstairs, Paul was crying for Emma. He was inconsolable and it was upsetting to watch. All the children missed her at first, but Paul's feelings of loss lasted longer.

'We spoke to Emma on the telephone and Paul enjoyed that, but he'd cry when the call ended. She came to visit us after a month and, although the visit was a success, afterwards Paul was really upset again for a couple of days. I realised that he had seen her too soon. Emma asked if she could come to a Halloween party that Anne was organising and I said, 'No. Paul isn't ready.' I felt mean, but I knew it was best for Paul and also for Anne. We had several more telephone conversations, and then Emma came to visit us before Christmas. It was now three months since she'd left. This time Paul recovered quicker, with the help of some chocolate for comfort. The following year, Emma came to all their birthday parties. We all enjoyed seeing her and each time the separation was easier. After about a year, Paul stopped crying when she left. After two years, we felt able to ask her to come on holiday with us to help us out. The children loved this, but didn't take it out on their current nanny on their return. We're still good friends and see her regularly. I'm sure we'll always keep in touch.'

Nanny perspective: Leaving

'I had been a live-in nanny for three children for three years. And in that time, I had become very close to every member of the family. Even though I agreed that it was time to move on, I still found it difficult to get motivated to find another nannying position. Towards the end of my employment, I started to feel some resentment towards the new nanny. Would she look after the children okay? It was hard knowing that I would have to let go and let someone else look after them.

'On my last day, I was an emotional wreck. As I took the children to school, I kept bursting into tears. I don't know if the children fully understood that I was leaving and would not look after them any more. Paul, the middle child, was a sensitive boy and we were very close. I found leaving him the hardest. As the end of my last day drew near, I found that I was constantly in tears and so was Paul. Eventually, I just had to say goodbye and go. After I'd left, I felt mixed up. I was upset to have left but also relieved that I could now move on and start afresh.'

ENDING IT WELL, WHEN IT'S GONE WRONG

When the separation is not mutual, the ending can be painful and messy. Both you and your nanny or au pair may feel let down and angry with each other.

After a cooling-off period, ask to have a chat with her. During your discussion, acknowledge that the relationship has deteriorated, and that you have both been hurt in the process. Express hope that you will both remember the good times, and that they won't be overshadowed by recent events. Wish her luck in the future.

Having had a positive discussion, you may both be able to move on and part on relatively good terms. This will benefit both of you, and more importantly, the children, who will be affected by any discord.

When you are dismissing your nanny without notice because of gross misconduct or asking your au pair to leave, it may be asking too much to part on good terms. However, even in those circumstances, try and end the relationship in a decent manner. Your departing nanny or au pair may choose to stay in the area, and it can be embarrassing for all of you, if you cannot be civil to each other.

SUMMARY

- When your nanny or au pair leaves, you and your children are likely to experience a sense of loss.
- When you are facing change, you need to be open and honest with each other about the reasons, so that you can try and rectify the situation or learn for the future.
- Discuss and agree a notice period, ideally of at least two months.
- You need to prepare the children for the change, to provide your departing nanny or au pair with a written reference, and to start recruiting a replacement.
- It is very important to celebrate the end together, in order to make the parting as happy as possible.
- Help your children to manage their loss by talking about it with them, and keeping in touch with your ex-nanny or old au pair.
- Even if the decision to part company is not mutual, try to ensure that you and your nanny or au pair part in a civil manner, to minimise future embarrassment for all concerned.

POSTSCRIPT

Some Words of Encouragement

Employers

"She's bubbly and happy and loves the children to bits. She's conscientious, willing, organised, caring and a good cook"

"She's firm but fair and creative with loads of energy. She thinks ahead and is honest, trustworthy and totally reliable"

Nannies

"They're a lovely family. They don't take advantage of me and I always finish on time. We work together so that the children have a great atmosphere to grow and develop in"

"I get on really well with my employers. The fact that they welcome my ideas means a lot to me"

Host families

"She's jolly, kind, flexible, noble, tough and kissable (quote from my daughter!)"

"She's a good timekeeper. She plays imaginatively with the children and has tons of patience. She's easy to live with and thorough with her cleaning. Her ironing is immaculate!"

Au pairs

"I love my family"

"My family is friendly, patient and helpful"

"I love learning the language and the culture and meeting new people with my family"

The children

"I like my nanny because she's good at cooking us pizza and prawns"
"She's cheerful and nice to us and very kind"
"She's good at comforting us"
"She makes me feel alright"
"She always smiles"

Comments and Questions

We hope you've found our book helpful and informative.

If you have any comments about the book, if you have experiences or tips that you would like to share with us, or if there are questions you would like to ask, you can visit our website – thenannyhandbook.com.

We'd love to hear from you.

Appendix I

DETAILS OF OUR SURVEY

Number of Respondents to the Questionnaire

Nannies	104
Employers of nannies	116
Au pairs	21
Host families	29

Age of nannies

Under 20	7%
20–25	41%
26–30	31%
31–35	15%
36 +	6%

Age of au pairs

Under 20	38%
20–27	62%

Length of job – nannies

Under 6 months	25%
6 months to one year	20%
1–2 years	28%
2–4 years	10%
4 years +	17%

Length of stay – au pairs

Up to 3 months	29%
3–6 months	33%
6–12 months	5%
12 months +	33%

Location of employers

Greater London	41%
Other	59%

Location of host families

Greater London	29%
Other	71%

Type of nanny

Live-in	27%
Live-out	73%

Appendix II

JOB DESCRIPTION FOR A LIVE-IN NANNY

Purpose of the job:
To look after the children and to ensure that all their emotional and physical needs are met while they are in your care.

Key responsibilities:

- To feed the children fresh, nutritious food. To make breakfast, lunch and tea for them and to provide snacks and drinks as appropriate. To ensure that they have a balanced diet and to limit the amount of sugar they eat.
- To dress the children and to make sure that they are clean and tidy in appearance.
- To wash, iron and mend the children's clothes.
- To change and wash the children's bedding and towels on a weekly basis, and more often if appropriate, e.g., if a child is ill or has an accident.
- To organise stimulating activities for the children, e.g., appropriate playgroups, visits to/from friends, arts, crafts and cooking at home, and outings to places of interest. To record all activities relating to the children in the diary so that we don't 'double-book' them.
- To ensure that the children get plenty of exercise and fresh air. When the children are in the garden, to supervise them and to ensure that they do not harm themselves on the play equipment.
- To encourage the children to tidy their bedrooms and put their clothes away, and to help them do so.
- To keep the kitchen, playroom and bathroom tidy, again encouraging the children to help. To sweep the kitchen floor on a daily basis and to load and unload the dishwasher and empty the kitchen bin when necessary.
- To plan menus for the week ahead and to prepare a weekly shopping list for your and the children's food. The list needs to be ready by Friday evening.

- To baby-sit twice a week for us. To put the children to bed at appropriate times, read them stories and go to them if they are distressed.
- To create a happy and relaxed environment around the children. To be loving and kind but also firm when required. To comfort them when they are sick or have injured themselves, to make them feel secure at all times.
- To drive the children to school and their activities carefully. To keep the car clean and tidy. In case of an accident or emergency, to ensure the safety of the children first, and then to take appropriate action to rectify the situation.
- To take the children to the doctor/hospital when they are sick. To visit the dentist and special clinics as necessary. To get their prescriptions, and to ensure that they take their medication.
- To liaise with the children's nursery and schools as required. To keep us informed about any issues, their progress and activities.
- To be responsible for the weekly float. To purchase food or clothing for the children as required. To pay the phone bill for your personal phone line on time and in full.
- To report all accidents and breakages to us as soon as possible, however minor.
- To oversee the children's homework, and make sure that they are not too exhausted to do it. To provide them with support while they are doing it.
- To accompany us on family outings, help out on birthdays, participate in family holidays and carry out proxy parenting (i.e., twenty-four-hour care) when required. To pack for the children when they are going away.
- To inform us at the end of each day about how the children have been and other relevant issues. To review how the job is going and provide us with open and honest feedback on a regular basis.

Appendix III

DAILY ROUTINE AND SCHEDULE OF WEEKLY ACTIVITIES

DAILY ROUTINE

Time	Activity
07.30–08.40	Children get up Elspeth has a bottle of milk and a cuddle before breakfast Children have breakfast Children get/are dressed, brush teeth and hair and take medication
08.00	Felix needs to be taken to the school bus (8.07 pick-up)
08.40	Leave for Wilfred's school (starts at 8.55) and Olivia's nursery (starts at 9.00)
09.15	Tidy up breakfast things Nursery duties Elspeth has morning sleep/activities*
11.45	Leave to pick Olivia up from nursery (12.00 pick-up)
12.30	Lunch
13.00	Olivia and Elspeth have afternoon rest/activities*
15.00	Leave to pick up Wilfred from school (15.20 pick-up) and Felix from school bus (15.30 pick-up)
15.50	Return home Activities* Homework
17.15	Tea
18.00	Baths Get into night clothes, brush teeth and hair and take medication

18.45	Homework (if done activities earlier)
	Video
	Elspeth has a bottle of milk
19.00	Parents take over!

**see schedule of weekly activities below*

SCHEDULE OF WEEKLY ACTIVITIES

Day	Time	Activity
Monday	08.40	Wilfred needs to take his weekly homework, lunch cheque and sports kit to school
	10.30–11.00	Elspeth to Waterbabies
	14.00–16.00	Olivia to art class
	17.30–18.00	Swimming classes
Tuesday	17.15–18.15	Wilfred to maths tutor
Wednesday	15.30–16.30	Wilfred does football after school
	16.00–16.30	Olivia to ballet class
Thursday	08.00	Felix needs to take his sports kit to school
	10.15–11.00	Elspeth to baby gym
Friday	08.40	Wilfred to return library book and take swim things to school
	09.15 onwards	Change children's sheets/wash towels

Appendix IV

SAMPLE CONTRACT FOR A LIVE-IN NANNY

PERSONAL DETAILS

Name of employer ________________________________

Employer's address ________________________________

Name of employee ________________________________

Employee's address ________________________________

Date of issue of contract ____________________________

Date of end of contract (if fixed term or temporary) __________

Date of commencement of employment ____________________

Previous service (if any) counting towards continuous employment

____

Job title ____

Place of work ______________________________________

Introduction

It is important that all contracts of employment operate on the basis of goodwill between the parties involved. Particularly where resident employment is concerned, it is vital that both parties accept and agree a degree of flexibility in the contract. However, to confirm the conditions of your engagement, we set out the details of your employment as required by law.

Remuneration

You will receive £X, payable weekly in arrears. Tax and National Insurance contributions will be paid on your weekly salary. We will ensure that on the day of payment you are given a payslip detailing your gross payment, deductions and net payment. Your salary will be reviewed on an annual basis, on the anniversary of your start date.

You will be provided with your own room (including a television and phone line), bathroom and kitchen. Your board includes all meals and use of the car, both when on and off duty.

Probationary period

The employee will be employed for a probationary period of one month.

Hours of work

Employment in a private household is such that it is difficult to define all hours of work and free time. However, your normal hours of work will be 8.00 am until 7.00 pm, and two evenings' baby-sitting a week. You will be allowed free weekends. If you are required to work additional hours, we will give you as much notice as possible, and compensate you with money or with time off in lieu. These hours can be changed only by mutual agreement.

Holidays

You will receive four weeks' paid holiday a year, plus all bank holidays. You are required to give us three months' notice of holidays, and are expected to take 50 per cent of your holidays at a time chosen by us (e.g., Christmas, Easter, etc.). The holiday year runs from X to X. In your final year of service, you will be entitled to holidays on a pro-rata basis. Holidays may only be carried into the next year with our permission.

Sickness

The employer will pay Statutory Sick Pay (SSP) at the rates stipulated by legislation. Your qualifying days will be Monday to Friday. We will pay you full pay for X weeks. After that period, SSP only will be due.

Termination

The first four weeks of employment will be probationary. In the first four weeks of employment, one week's notice is required on either side. After four weeks' continuous service, either the employee or the employer may terminate this contract by giving four weeks' notice. After two years' continuous employment, there will be one week's additional notice for each year of continuous employment, up to a maximum of twelve weeks.

Confidentiality

It is a condition of employment that now, and at all times in the future, the employee keeps secret the affairs and concerns of the household and its transactions and business. Therefore, all conversations and information in any way connected with us are to be treated as confidential.

Pension

The employer does not run a pension scheme.

Discipline

Reasons which might give rise to the need for disciplinary action include the following:

- being a disruptive influence in the house;
- job incompetence;
- unsatisfactory standard of dress or appearance;
- breach of the confidentiality clause;
- conduct during or outside working hours prejudicial to the interest or reputation of the employer;
- unreliability in time-keeping or attendance; and
- failure to comply with instructions and procedure, e.g. being unable to drive because of a driving ban.

In the event of the need to take disciplinary action, the procedure will be:

1 oral warning;
2 written warning; and
3 dismissal.

You have the right to appeal to an agreed third party (see grievance procedure below).

Reasons which might give rise to summary dismissal include theft, placing the children in danger, illegal drug-taking, drunkenness, child abuse and failure to disclose all relevant information at your interview.

GRIEVANCE PROCEDURE

If you have any concerns, problems or grievances about your employment, please raise them promptly with us. Should a serious grievance arise, you have the right to seek advice. [You need to agree and state who this third party is: family solicitor, doctor, nanny agency, etc.]

SIGNATURES

I agree to abide by the terms and conditions set out in this contract.

Signed by employer____________________ Date______________

Signed by employee____________________ Date______________

Appendix V

PACKING LIST

Wilfred and Felix

Pants
Socks
Tops/shirts
Trousers/shorts
Jumpers/sweatshirts
Shoes/trainers
Wellingtons/beach shoes
Slippers
Dressing gowns
Pyjamas
Comfort toys
Hats
Gloves
Swim things, including goggles
Coats
Belts
Toys and books
Homework
Hairbrush
Shampoo
Toothbrushes and toothpaste
Scissors
Medicines: e.g., inhalers and eczema cream, Calpol for 6 years +
Bikes
Sun cream
Sports kit

Olivia

Pants
Tights/socks
Tops/shirts
Trousers
Jumpers/cardigans
Dresses/skirts
Shoes/trainers
Wellingtons/beach shoes
Slippers
Dressing gown
Nightclothes
Comfort toys
Muslins
Coat
Gloves
Hair bands/accessories
Swim things, including goggles
Toys and books
Toothbrush and toothpaste
Any medicine?

Elspeth

Nappies/nappy sacks/wipes
Nightclothes
Sleep suit
Muslins
Outfits
Vests
Tights/socks
Shoes
Cardigans
Coat
Hat
Gloves
Bibs and spoons
Bottles
Buggy and rain cover/parasol
Travel cot and duvet
Kit bag, including changing mat
Backpack
Toys and books
Monitor
Comfort toys
Medicines: e.g., Calpol, Bongela

Appendix VI

SAMPLE REFERENCES FOR A NANNY

REFERENCE FOR A GOOD NANNY

Susan Blott worked for me for two years, from [date] to [date]. We had a nanny-share arrangement at the time, with another family. She looked after my son, George (5 months), and a baby girl, Edwina (9 months).

Susan was an excellent nanny, particularly for young children. She established a good routine for the children within a few days of joining us. Susan cooked healthy meals for the children and organised suitable activities. She took them out for walks, found fun playgroups for them and played creatively with them at home. She advised us on appropriate toys and music to buy to stimulate the children. George was very happy and secure in her care.

She kept the house tidy, was punctual, and had very little time off sick. Susan was also good company and easy to be around. She drove our car and was a safe driver. We all missed her a lot when she left.

REFERENCE FOR A POOR NANNY

Elaine Williams was employed as our nanny from [date] to [date]. She looked after our son, Freddy (13 months), and daughter, Carmella (3 years).

Elaine had sole charge of the children. She selected playgroups for them and found them local playmates of a similar age. She planned menus and cooked their food on a daily basis. Elaine carried out the nursery duties too. She was always firm with the children.

The job was a live-in post. During the year we moved house and then embarked on various DIY projects in our new home. Elaine was quite flexible about her changing living conditions.

Overall, we were relatively happy with the way in which Elaine looked after the children.

Useful Contacts

BTEC Information Service 020–7393 4444
(For information about child-care qualifications)

City & Guilds 020–7294 2468
(For information about child-care qualifications)

Council for Awards in Child Care and Education (CACHE) 01727–847 636
(For information about child-care qualifications)

Employer's Help Line 0845–714 3143
New Employer's Help Line 0845–607 0143
(For tax, National Insurance, SSP and SMP queries)

Julie Skinner 'Special People' 020–7372 9504
(Nanny agency which places experienced nannies to work with children with special needs)

Maternity Alliance 020–7588 8582
(For information on maternity rights and services)

Nanny Payroll Service 01536–373 111
(Payroll service for the employers of nannies)

Nanny Share Network 020–8516 5948
(For parents and nannies seeking/offering shared child care (part-time and full-time) in and around London)

Nanny Tax 01273–626 256
(Payroll service for employers of nannies)

National Vocational Qualifications (NVQs and SVQs) 020–7286 6600 (NVQs)
(For information about child-care qualifications) 0141–248 7900 (SVQs)

Nursery World 020–7782 3000
(Weekly magazine suitable for placing advertisements for nannies)

Parents at Work 020–7628 3565
(Provides parents with help and advice about child care)

Professional Association of Nursery Nurses (PANN) 01332–372 337
(For information and advice on any aspect of employing a nanny) www.pat.org.uk

The Chiltern College 0118–947 1847
(Specialist nanny college)

The Home Office 0870–6067766
(For information about au pairs) www.homeoffice.gov.uk

The International Au Pair Association (IAPA) 00–45–33 33 9600
(Organisation set up to help to regulate au pair agencies) www.iapa.org

The Lady 020–7379 4717
(Weekly magazine suitable for placing advertisements for nannies and au pairs)

The London Montessori Centre 020–7493 0165
(Specialist centre for child-care qualifications)

The National Childbirth Trust (NCT) 020–8992 8637
(For information about nanny share registers in your area)

The Norland College 01488–682252
(Specialist nanny college)

The Princess Christian College 0161–224 4560
(Specialist nanny college)

The Recruitment and Employment Federation (REC) 020–7323 4300
(Organisation set up to help to regulate nanny and au pair agencies) www.rec.uk.com

Index